# Credit control

## Workbook

**Alison Aplin**
**Michael Fardon**

Published by Osborne Books Limited
Unit 1B Everoak Estate
Bromyard Road, Worcester WR2 5HP
Tel 01905 748071
Email books@osbornebooks.co.uk
Website www.osbornebooks.co.uk

Design by Laura Ingham

Printed by CPI Group (UK) Limited, Croydon, CRO 4YY, on environmentally friendly, acid-free paper from managed forests.

British Library Cataloguing in Publication Data
A catalogue record for this book is available from the British Library

ISBN 978 1909173 415

# Contents

## Chapter activities

# Acknowledgements

The publisher wishes to thank Jon Moore and Cathy Turner for their help with the reading and production of the book. Thanks are also due to Jo Osborne, Aubrey Penning and Tom Fardon for their technical editing and to Laura Ingham for her designs for this new series.

The publisher is indebted to the Association of Accounting Technicians for its help and advice to our authors and editors during the preparation of this text.

# Author

**Alison Aplin** is the owner of an accountancy practice which specialises in small businesses. She is a chartered management accountant, a member of AAT, and has worked in industry, practice and education. Alison also has extensive writing and teaching experience, predominantly in the areas of financial accounting and taxation.

**Michael Fardon** has extensive teaching experience of a wide range of banking, business and accountancy courses at Worcester College of Technology. He now specialises in writing business and financial texts and is General Editor at Osborne Books. He is also an educational consultant and has worked extensively in the areas of vocational business curriculum development.

# Introduction

## what this book covers

This book has been written to cover the 'Credit control' Unit which is an optional Unit for the revised (2013) AAT Level 4 Diploma in Accounting.

## what this book contains

This book is set out in two sections:

- **Chapter Activities** which provide extra practice material in addition to the activities included in the Osborne Books Tutorial text. Answers to the Chapter activities are included in this book.

- **Practice Assessments** are provided to prepare the student for the Computer Based Assessments. They are based directly on the structure, style and content of the sample assessment material provided by the AAT at www.aat.org.uk. Suggested answers to the Practice Assessments are set out in this book.

## further information

If you want to know more about our products and resources, please visit www.osbornebooks.co.uk for further details and access to our online shop.

# Chapter activities

# 1 Introduction to credit control

**1.1** Your business is experiencing difficulty in extracting payment from one of your top company customers with whom your company communicates on a daily basis. Which **one** of the following options is the best way of obtaining up-to-date information about the customer's credit standing?

✔

| | | |
|---|---|---|
| (a) | Reading trade magazines | |
| (b) | A search for the company's accounts at Companies House | |
| (c) | Talking to your colleagues in the sales and accounts departments | |

Tick the **one** correct option.

**1.2** Management accounts are useful in the assessment of a limited company's credit standing because they provide information about:

✔

| | | |
|---|---|---|
| (a) | Guarantees given by the directors, share ownership, profitability | |
| (b) | Management structure, credit insurance cover, bank balance | |
| (c) | Profitability, credit insurance cover, gearing | |
| (d) | Liquidity, profitability, sales revenue | |

Tick the **one** correct option.

**1.3** Information about a company received from a credit reference agency can include: ✔

| | | |
|---|---|---|
| (a) | Financial accounts, payment history, records of any court proceedings | |
| (b) | Financial accounts, bank references, directors' bank details | |
| (c) | Financial accounts, trade references, employee credit histories | |

Tick the **one** correct option.

**1.4** You are assessing an application for a trading credit limit of £25,000 with one month terms from a new customer, Tufnell Services Limited. You have received the bank reference and two trade references shown below.

You are to read the references, assess them for risk and complete the table below. You are asked to identify the significant wording in each reference which will guide your assessment of the risk involved.

---

## Aurum Bank PLC

**status report: Tufnell Services Limited**

**Request:** £25,000 trade credit

**Report:** The capital of this company is fully employed, but we do not consider the directors would enter into any commitment they could not meet.

---

### Response to trade credit enquiry, received from Hensall & Co

**Re: Tufnell Limited: £25,000 trade credit, terms one month**

We have been trading with this company for two years and allow £15,000 credit per month on 60 day terms. The company very occasionally exceeds the 60 days.

---

### Response to trade credit enquiry, received from R Wagner Associates

**Tufnell Limited: £25,000 credit per month**

We have been trading with this customer for over six years and now allow them £10,000 credit per month on 60 day terms. The account is usually paid on time.

---

| Reference received | Risk rating | | | Significant wording |
|---|---|---|---|---|
| | high ✔ | medium ✔ | low ✔ | |
| Aurum Bank PLC | | | | |
| Hensall & Co | | | | |
| R Wagner Associates | | | | |

# 2 Financial analysis of customer accounts

**2.1** Set out below and on the next page are the financial statements for Le Ann Limited.

**Le Ann Limited: Statement of Profit or Loss**

|  | 20X3 | 20X2 |
|---|---|---|
|  | *£000* | *£000* |
| Sales revenue | 6,700 | 6,250 |
| Cost of sales | 4,690 | 4,250 |
| Gross profit | 2,010 | 2,000 |
| Distribution costs | 203 | 185 |
| Administration expenses | 1,003 | 877 |
| Profit from operations | 804 | 938 |
| Finance costs | 16 | 13 |
| Profit before taxation | 788 | 925 |
| Taxation | 140 | 180 |
| Profit for the year | 648 | 745 |

The above figures include:

20X3 Depreciation £36,000

20X2 Depreciation £28,000

**Le Ann Limited: Statement of Financial Position**

|  | 20X3 | 20X2 |
|---|---|---|
|  | £000 | £000 |
| **ASSETS** |  |  |
| **Non-current assets** |  |  |
| Property, plant and equipment | 733 | 583 |
|  |  |  |
| **Current assets** |  |  |
| Inventories | 963 | 873 |
| Trade and other receivables | 1,138 | 1,113 |
| Cash | 11 | 25 |
|  | 2,112 | 2,011 |
| **Total assets** | 2,845 | 2,594 |
|  |  |  |
| **EQUITY AND LIABILITIES** |  |  |
| **Equity** |  |  |
| Share capital | 1,500 | 1,500 |
| Retained earnings | 359 | 258 |
| **Total equity** | 1,859 | 1,758 |
|  |  |  |
| **Non-current liabilities** |  |  |
| Borrowing | 250 | 150 |
|  |  |  |
| **Current liabilities** |  |  |
| Borrowings | 56 | 76 |
| Trade and other payables | 680 | 610 |
| **Total liabilities** | 986 | 836 |
| **Total equity and liabilities** | 2,845 | 2,594 |

**(a)** Calculate the liquidity key indicators (to 2 decimal places) for 20X3 and 20X2 for Le Ann Limited:

| Le Ann Limited | 20X3 Indicator | 20X2 Indicator |
|---|---|---|
| Current ratio | | |
| Quick ratio | | |
| Trade receivables collection period in days | | |
| Trade payables payment period in days | | |
| Inventory holding period in days | | |

**(b)** Calculate the profitability key indicators (to 2 decimal places) for 20X3 and 20X2 for Le Ann Limited:

| Le Ann Limited | 20X3 Indicator | 20X2 Indicator |
|---|---|---|
| Gross profit margin % | | |
| Profit from operations margin % | | |
| Interest cover | | |
| Return on capital employed % | | |

**(c)** Calculate the debt key indicators (to 2 decimal places) for 20X3 and 20X2 for Le Ann Limited:

| Le Ann Limited | 20X3 Indicator | 20X2 Indicator |
|---|---|---|
| Gearing % | | |
| Short-term debt % | | |
| EBITDA / total debt | | |

(EBITDA = Earnings before interest, tax, depreciation and amortisation)

**2.2** The credit rating (scoring) system below is used to assess the risk of default from credit customers by calculating key indicators (ratios):

| Credit rating (scoring) system | Score |
|---|---|
| **Profit from operations margin** | |
| Losses | –5 |
| Less than 5% | 0 |
| 5% and above but less than 10% | 5 |
| 10% and above but less than 20% | 10 |
| 20% or more | 20 |
| **Interest cover** | |
| No cover | –30 |
| Less than 1 | –20 |
| 1 and above but less than 2 | –10 |
| 2 and above but less than 4 | 0 |
| 4 or more | 10 |
| **Liquidity ratio** | |
| Less than 1 | –20 |
| 1 and above but less than 1.25 | –10 |
| 1.25 and above but less than 1.5 | 0 |
| 1.5 or more | 10 |
| **Gearing (total debt / total debt plus equity)** | |
| Less than 25% | 20 |
| 25% and above but less than 50% | 10 |
| 50% and above but less than 65% | 0 |
| 65% and above but less than 75% | –20 |
| 75% and above but less than 80% | –40 |
| 80% or more | –100 |

| Risk | Aggregate score |
|---|---|
| Very low risk | Between 60 and 21 |
| Low risk | Between 20 and 1 |
| Medium risk | Between 0 and –24 |
| High risk | Between –25 and –50 |
| Very high risk | Between –50 and –160 |

**(a)** Calculate the total credit rating for each year for the company below by completing the ratings columns in the table:

| Belfast Cherries Limited | 20X3 Indicator | 20X3 Rating | 20X2 Indicator | 20X2 Rating |
|---|---|---|---|---|
| Profit from operations margin % | 6% | | 3.5% | |
| Interest cover | 1.5 | | None | |
| Quick ratio | 1.1 | | 0.9 | |
| Gearing % | 55% | | 59% | |
| Total credit rating | | | | |

**(b)** Based on the results of your credit rating and using the table below, recommend whether a requested credit limit should be given to Belfast Cherries Limited.

Tick your chosen option in the table at the bottom of the page.

| Rating | Decision |
|---|---|
| Very low or low risk current year and very low or low risk previous year | Accept |
| Very low or low risk current year and medium risk previous year | Accept |
| Very low or low risk current year and high or very high risk previous year | Request latest management accounts and defer decision |
| Very high risk or high risk current year | Reject |
| Medium risk current year and medium, low or very low risk previous year | Accept |
| Medium risk current year and high or very high risk previous year | Request latest management accounts and defer decision |

| Customer | Decision | ✔ |
|---|---|---|
| Belfast Cherries Limited | Accept | |
| | Reject | |
| | Request latest management accounts and defer decision | |

# 3 Granting credit and setting up customer accounts

**3.1** Clarke Limited has been trading with Peacock Limited for several years and has, until recently, always paid to terms. Following several late payments Clarke Limited has now contacted Peacock Limited to request an increase in its credit limit from £50,000 to £100,000.

Clarke Limited has supplied the Statement of Profit or Loss and the Statement of Financial Position shown below and on the next page.

### Clarke Limited: Statement of Profit or Loss

|  | 20X2 | 20X1 |
| --- | --- | --- |
|  | £000 | £000 |
| Sales revenue | 4,705 | 3,764 |
| Cost of sales | 2,087 | 1,355 |
| Gross profit | 2,618 | 2,409 |
| Distribution costs | 329 | 188 |
| Administration expenses | 2,485 | 1,920 |
| Profit / (loss) from operations | (196) | 301 |
| Finance costs | 38 | 20 |
| Profit / (loss) before taxation | (234) | 281 |
| Taxation | - | 50 |
| Profit / (loss) for the year | (234) | 231 |

**Clarke Limited: Statement of Financial Position**

|  | 20X2 | 20X1 |
|---|---|---|
|  | *£000* | *£000* |
| **ASSETS** | | |
| **Non-current assets** | | |
| Property, plant and equipment | 1,030 | 1,050 |
|  | | |
| **Current assets** | | |
| Inventories | 240 | 241 |
| Trade and other receivables | 928 | 619 |
| Cash | - | 11 |
|  | 1,168 | 871 |
| **Total assets** | **2,198** | **1,921** |
|  | | |
| **EQUITY AND LIABILITIES** | | |
| **Equity** | | |
| Share capital | 850 | 850 |
| Retained earnings | 16 | 250 |
| **Total equity** | **866** | **1,100** |
|  | | |
| **Non-current liabilities** | | |
| Borrowing | 750 | 650 |
|  | | |
| **Current liabilities** | | |
| Bank overdraft | 159 | - |
| Trade and other payables | 423 | 171 |
| **Total liabilities** | **1,332** | **821** |
| **Total equity and liabilities** | **2,198** | **1,921** |

Peacock Limited has calculated financial indicators from the financial statements provided by Clarke Limited.

These indicators are shown at the top of the next page.

| Clarke Limited | 20X2 | 20X1 |
|---|---|---|
| Gross profit margin % | 55.64 | 64 |
| Profit from operations margin % | −4.17 | 8 |
| Interest cover | None | 15.05 |
| Current ratio | 2.01 | 5.09 |
| Trade payables payment period in days | 73.98 | 46.06 |
| Trade receivables collection period in days | 71.99 | 60.03 |
| Inventory holding period in days | 41.97 | 64.92 |
| Gearing % | 51.21 | 37.14 |

The Sales Manager of Peacock Limited has reviewed the financial statements provided by Clarke Limited and the financial indicators shown above and has made some comments.

**You are to** write bullet point notes dealing with each comment that the Sales Manager has made in (a) to (j) below.

**(a)** The company turnover has increased by 20% from £3,764,000 to £4,705,000. This is a clear sign of overtrading.

**(b)** The gross profit has increased, which is a good sign.

**(c)**     The profit from operations has decreased by £196,000. This means that less cash is available to pay debts.

**(d)**     The interest cover has decreased which means that the company is in a worse position than last year.

**(e)**     The current ratio should be 2 which means that last year it was too high.

**(f)** The trade receivables have increased by 50% which supports the conclusion of overtrading.

**(g)** The trade payables have increased by £252,000 which indicates the company is not paying its suppliers and requires the increase in the credit limit.

**(h)** The inventory has remained the same which is a good sign.

**(i)** The total funding (equity and borrowing) has only increased by £25,000 which is a good sign.

**(j)** My conclusion is that credit should be given.

# 4 Customer accounts – legal aspects

**4.1**   All valid contracts contain the following four elements:

✔

| | | |
|---|---|---|
| (a) | Offer, acceptance, specific performance, consideration | |
| (b) | Offer, acceptance, consideration, an intention to create legal relations | |
| (c) | Offer, acceptance, termination date, implied terms | |

Tick the **one** correct option.

**4.2**   The term 'subject to contract' in relation to a written contract of sale for goods means that:

✔

| | | |
|---|---|---|
| (a) | The contract has been agreed and signed but the goods have not yet been delivered to the buyer | |
| (b) | The contract is unsigned but is now binding on the buyer and seller | |
| (c) | The terms of the contract have not yet been agreed between the parties – there is an ongoing discussion about the price | |
| (d) | The buyer has agreed in principle to all the terms of the contract but the contract has not yet been drawn up | |

Tick the **one** correct option.

**4.3** The Sale of Goods Act states that goods sold must be: ✔

| (a) | Manufactured to a very high standard | |
|---|---|---|
| (b) | As described | |
| (c) | Of satisfactory quality | |
| (d) | Sold at the advertised price | |

Tick the **two** correct options.

**4.4** Which of the following constitutes an acceptance of an offer in contract: ✔

| (a) | 'I agree to buy goods from you, but I insist on 15% trade discount' | |
|---|---|---|
| (b) | 'I agree to buy goods from you and will accept your stated terms and conditions' | |
| (c) | 'I agree to buy this property from you, subject to contract' | |

Tick the **one** correct option.

**4.5** John agrees to buy Mike's car for £1,000. Nothing is set down in writing. John takes possession of the car but then finds that he does not have the money to pay for the car. Magda, John's partner, agrees to pay the £1,000 as she has recently won £5,000 on the Lottery. The car is then sold but turns out to be unroadworthy and only worth £200. John wants to get his money back. The legal position is as follows: ✔

| (a) | John cannot sue Mike because the £1,000 consideration was paid by Magda | |
|---|---|---|
| (b) | John cannot sue Mike because the £1,000 consideration was greater than the actual value of the car | |
| (c) | John cannot sue Mike because the contract was not in writing | |

Tick the **one** correct option.

**4.6** A person who takes legal action in the courts for compensation for a contract where the work has not been completed will seek the remedy of:

✔

| | | |
|---|---|---|
| (a) | Satisfactory performance | |
| (b) | Specific performance | |
| (c) | Repeat performance | |

Tick the **one** correct option.

**4.7** The Late Payments of Commercial Debts (Interest) Act allows small companies to charge interest to customers who exceed their credit terms and pay late. The interest charge is based on the current bank base rate.

**You are to** enter in the box below the percentage rate charged.

If the current base rate is 1.5%, the late payment interest rate is ⬚ per cent.

**4.8** A customer owes £8,000 (excluding VAT @ 20%) and the debt is 75 days late.

**You are to** calculate the interest charge under the Late Payments of Commercial Debts (Interest) Act to the nearest penny. Enter the figure in the box below. The bank base rate is 1.25%.

£ ⬚

# 5 Monitoring and controlling customer accounts

**5.1** The sales ledger account for Dido Ltd has become corrupted but the following information is available:

Account balance 1 January 20X3: £78,000

Invoices raised: 10 January 20X3 £45,000 plus VAT at 20%

12 February 20X3 £26,400 (VAT inclusive)

Credit notes raised: 16 January 20X3 £2,760 (VAT inclusive) subject to a restocking fee of 10%

Bank receipts: 18 January 20X3 £75,240

26 February 20X3 £45,000

**You are to** balance the account of Dido Ltd as at 31 January 20X3 and 28 February 20X3.

**5.2**  You have been provided with the credit control procedures for Singer Limited. Today's date is 31 August 20X3.

---

**Credit control procedures**

1.  An order for goods is received by email, fax or phone (all phone calls are recorded).

2.  Goods are delivered and a goods received note is signed by the customer.

3.  The goods received notes are kept in a file in the accounts office.

4.  An invoice will be issued on the day after delivery on 30 day terms.

5.  An aged analysis of trade receivables is produced weekly.

6.  A statement is sent when the account is 7 days overdue.

7.  When a debt is 14 days overdue a reminder telephone call is made.

8.  When a debt is 21 days overdue a final reminder letter is sent.

9.  When a debt is 28 days overdue the account will be put on stop.

10. The debt will either be placed in the hands of a debt collection company or legal proceedings could be instigated if the customer does not respond to calls or letters.

11. The business is credit insured, however insurance is only given for customers once they have a history of trade with the business of at least 12 months and have successfully paid for at least three invoiced amounts. Only 80% of the value of the debt is insured. VAT will be reclaimed from HMRC.

---

The assistant responsible for credit control has been on sick leave for several months but you have access to the company credit control procedures.

Set out below is an extract from the aged trade receivables analysis at 31 August 20X3.

| Customer | Balance £ | 0 – 30 days £ | 31 – 60 days £ | 61 – 90 days £ | Over 90 days £ |
|---|---|---|---|---|---|
| Baritone Ltd | 88,800 | 38,400 | 50,400 | | |
| Bass Ltd | 12,720 | | 12,720 | | |
| Contralto Ltd | 18,000 | | | | 18,000 |
| Soprano Ltd | 17,400 | | | | 17,400 |
| Tenor Ltd | 39,516 | 34,440 | | 5,076 | |

**You are to** identify the most appropriate course of action for each customer based on the information provided. See the next two pages for details of the customers.

### Baritone Ltd

The balance on Baritone Ltd's account consists of two invoices. An unallocated payment has been received for £50,400 and posted to the unallocated payment accounts in the purchase ledger. It has now been identified as a receipt from Baritone Ltd.

The action needed is (tick the correct option):

✔

| | | |
|---|---|---|
| (a) | Credit Baritone Ltd's account with £50,400 and debit unallocated payments with £50,400 | |
| (b) | Debit Baritone Ltd's account with £50,400 and debit unallocated payments with £50,400 | |
| (c) | Credit Baritone Ltd's account with £50,400 and credit unallocated payments with £50,400 | |
| (d) | Debit Baritone Ltd's account with £50,400 and credit unallocated payments with £50,400 | |

### Bass Ltd

The balance on Bass Ltd's account consists of one invoice dated 23 July 20X3.

The action needed is (tick the correct option):

✔

| | | |
|---|---|---|
| (a) | The account should be put on stop | |
| (b) | The account is not overdue so no action is required | |
| (c) | A final reminder letter should be sent on 5 September 20X3 | |
| (d) | A statement should have been sent on 29 August 20X3 | |

### Contralto Ltd

Contralto Ltd has gone into administration. The account is credit insured.

The action needed is (tick the correct option):

✔

| | | |
|---|---|---|
| (a) | Place the account on stop and contact a debt collection company to deal with processing a claim against Contralto Ltd | |
| (b) | Contact the insolvency service and register a claim with the credit insurer | |
| (c) | Contact the insolvency practitioner and register a claim with the credit insurer | |
| (d) | Contact the insolvency practitioner and make a provision in the accounts | |

**Soprano Ltd**

The account for Soprano Ltd is on stop. Attempts to contact the customer by telephone have been unsuccessful. The account is credit insured.

Complete the sentence below by inserting the correct figures:

Contact the credit insurer to make a claim for £ [          ]

Make a provision for £ [          ]

Claim VAT of £ [          ] from HMRC.

**Tenor Ltd**

The amount of £5,076 is for one invoice. Tenor Ltd claims that the goods were not received, but there is a signed delivery note on the file.

The action needed is to (tick the correct option):

|  |  | ✔ |
|---|---|---|
| (a) | Send the original delivery note signed by Tenor Ltd | |
| (b) | Raise a credit note for £5,076 | |
| (c) | Send a copy of the signed delivery note which was signed by Tenor Ltd | |
| (d) | Put the account on stop | |

**5.3** A small business has a large company customer that is very behind with settling its account. What statute will help the seller encourage earlier settlement of invoices?

Tick the **one** appropriate option.

| | | ✔ |
|---|---|---|
| (a) | Consumer Credit Act | |
| (b) | Late Payment of Commercial Debts (Interest) Act | |
| (c) | Insolvency Act | |

**5.4** A business that wishes to use a service which will remove the risk of losses made through customers becoming insolvent is most likely to use which of the following services?

Tick the **one** appropriate option.

| | | ✔ |
|---|---|---|
| (a) | A credit insurance company | |
| (b) | A credit reference agency | |
| (c) | A firm of solicitors | |

**5.5** Tribbiani Ltd is a regular customer of Ross Ltd. During the year Tribbiani Ltd bought from Ross Ltd 495 items which cost £175 each, including VAT at 20%. At the end of the year Tribbiani Ltd's balance of account was £14,438.

The receivables collection period (to the nearest day) is: [          ] days.

# 6 Collecting debts and dealing with insolvency

**6.1** A business has a £35,000 debt outstanding on a customer account. Which County Court process deals with this size of debt?

Tick the **one** correct option.

| | | ✔ |
|---|---|---|
| (a) | Small Claims Track | |
| (b) | Fast Track | |
| (c) | Multi Track | |

**6.2** An attachment of earnings is:

Tick the **one** correct option.

| | | ✔ |
|---|---|---|
| (a) | An order for the court bailiffs to enter the property of the customer who owes money to the seller to seize valuable assets | |
| (b) | An order which will authorise an employer to deduct regular amounts from the customer's salary in order to repay the debt | |
| (c) | An order which will give the seller a right to the sale proceeds of property owned by the customer | |

**6.3** A statutory demand made on a trade receivable for an outstanding debt should be for a minimum of:

Tick the **one** correct option.

| | | ✔ |
|---|---|---|
| (a) | £500 | |
| (b) | £750 | |
| (c) | £1,000 | |

**6.4** A 'retention of title' clause in a sales contract for goods supplied means that a business that has sold goods but not received payment for them can recover the goods if the buyer becomes insolvent. But the clause will only operate under certain conditions.

Which **one** of the following situations will allow a seller which has incorporated a retention of title clause in its contract to recover the goods?

Tick the correct option.

| | | ✔ |
|---|---|---|
| (a) | The goods can be identified as having been supplied by the seller, for example with a stamp or label | |
| (b) | The goods have been used in a manufacturing process and mixed with other products | |
| (c) | The goods have been in the possession of the buyer for less than 60 days | |

**6.5** You work in the Credit Control Section for Lewis Enterprises, which is owed £10,000 by Brodey Ltd, which has recently been put into liquidation. Brodey Ltd's trade payables total £250,000.

You receive a schedule from the court stating that £500,000 has been realised from the sale of the company's assets. The payables that will receive payment from this are:

Payables to be paid **in full** are:

| Liquidation costs and preferential payables | £150,000 |
|---|---|
| Bank floating charge | £200,000 |

**You are to calculate**:

**(1)** The dividend (pence per £1) payable to the trade payables: [        ] pence.

**(2)** The amount that will be received by Lewis Enterprises: £[        ]

**(3)** The amount that will be written off as an irrecoverable debt: £[        ]

Ignore any VAT.

# Chapter activities answers

# 1 Introduction to credit control

**1.1** (c) Talking to your colleagues in the sales and accounts departments

**1.2** (d) Liquidity, profitability, sales revenue

**1.3** (a) Financial accounts, payment history, records of any court proceedings

**1.4**

| Reference received | Risk rating | | | Significant wording |
|---|---|---|---|---|
| | **high** | **medium** | **low** | |
| Aurum Bank PLC | ✔ | | | The capital of this company is **fully** employed. |
| Hensall & Co | | ✔ | | **very occasionally** exceeds |
| R Wagner Associates | | ✔ | | The account is **usually** paid on time. |

# 2 Financial analysis of customer accounts

**2.1** (a)

| Le Ann Limited | 20X3 Indicator | 20X2 Indicator |
|---|---|---|
| Current ratio | 2.87 | 2.93 |
| Quick ratio | 1.56 | 1.66 |
| Trade receivables collection period in days | 62 | 65 |
| Trade payables payment period in days | 52.92 | 52.39 |
| Inventory holding period in days | 74.95 | 74.98 |

**Workings:**

| | Formula | 20X3 | 20X2 |
|---|---|---|---|
| Current ratio | Current assets / Current liabilities | 2,112 / (56 + 680) = 2.87 | 2,011 / (76 + 610) = 2.93 |
| Quick ratio | Current assets less inventories / Current liabilities | (2,112 – 963) / (56 + 680) = 1.56 | (2,011 – 873) / (76 + 610) = 1.66 |
| Trade receivables collection period in days | Trade receivables x 365 / Sales revenue | 1,138 x 365 / 6,700 = 62 | 1,113 x 365 / 6,250 = 65 |
| Trade payable pmt period in days | Trade payables x 365 / Cost of sales | 680 x 365 / 4,690 = 52.92 | 610 x 365 / 4,250 = 52.39 |
| Inventory holding period in days | Inventories x 365 / Cost of sales | 963 x 365 / 4,690 = 74.95 | 873 x 365 / 4,250 = 74.98 |

**(b)**

| Le Ann Limited | 20X3 Indicator | 20X2 Indicator |
|---|---|---|
| Gross profit margin % | 30 | 32 |
| Profit from operations margin % | 12 | 15.01 |
| Interest cover | 50.25 | 72.15 |
| Return on capital employed % | 38.12 | 49.16 |

**Workings:**

| | Formula | 20X3 | 20X2 |
|---|---|---|---|
| Gross profit margin % | Gross profit x 100 / Sales revenue | 2,010 x 100 / 6,700 = 30% | 2,000 x 100 / 6,250 = 32% |
| Profit from operations margin % | Profit from operations x 100 / Sales revenue | 804 x 100 / 6,700 = 12% | 938 x 100 / 6,250 = 15.01% |
| Interest cover | Profit from operations / Interest payable | 804 / 16 = 50.25 | 938 / 13 = 72.15 |
| Return on capital employed % | Profit from operations x 100 / Net assets | 804 x 100 / (2,845 – 736) = 38.12% | 938 x 100 / (2,594 – 686) = 49.16% |

**(c)**

| Le Ann Limited | 20X3 Indicator | 20X2 Indicator |
|---|---|---|
| Gearing % | 14.13 | 11.39 |
| Short-term debt % | 18.30 | 33.63 |
| EBITDA / total debt | 2.75 | 4.27 |

**Workings**:

| | Formula | 20X3 | 20X2 |
|---|---|---|---|
| Gearing % | $\dfrac{\text{Total debt} \times 100}{\text{Total debt plus equity}}$ | $\dfrac{306 \times 100}{306 + 1,859} = 14.13\%$ | $\dfrac{226 \times 100}{226 + 1,758} = 11.39\%$ |
| Short-term debt % | $\dfrac{\text{Short-term debt} \times 100}{\text{Total debt}}$ | $\dfrac{56 \times 100}{56 + 250} = 18.30\%$ | $\dfrac{76 \times 100}{76 + 150} = 33.63\%$ |
| EBITDA / total debt | $\dfrac{\text{EBITDA} \times 100}{\text{Total debt}}$ | $\dfrac{804 + 36}{56 + 250} = 2.75$ | $\dfrac{938 + 28}{150 + 76} = 4.27$ |

**2.2    (a)**

| Belfast Cherries Limited | 20X3 Indicator | 20X3 Rating | 20X2 Indicator | 20X2 Rating |
|---|---|---|---|---|
| Profit from operations margin % | 6% | 5 | 3.5% | 0 |
| Interest cover | 1.5 | −10 | None | −30 |
| Quick ratio | 1.1 | −10 | 0.9 | −20 |
| Gearing % | 55% | 0 | 59% | 0 |
| Total credit rating | | −15 | | −50 |

**(b)**    Request latest management accounts and defer decision

# 3  Granting credit and setting up customer accounts

**3.1**   **(a)**   **The company turnover has increased by 20% from £3,764,000 to £4,705,000. This is a clear sign of overtrading.**

- It is correct that the turnover has increased; however, the increase is 25% (£941,000 / £3,764,000) not 20%.

- The fact that turnover has increased may be a sign of overtrading, but other factors must be taken into consideration.

- Other indicators of overtrading include reduced profit margins, increased levels of current assets and trade cycle days and the reduction in cashflow.

**(b)**   **The gross profit has increased, which is a good sign.**

- There has been an increase in gross profit from £2,409,000 to £2,618,000; however the gross profit margin has fallen from 64% to 55.64%, which is not a good sign.

- The fall in the gross profit margin may indicate that suppliers have increased their prices or the company is not taking advantage of early settlement discounts on offer. It may also indicate that the company has reduced its prices.

**(c)**   **The profit from operations has decreased by £196,000. This means that less cash is available to pay debts.**

- The profit from operations has decreased and is now an operating loss, it has fallen by £497,000, not £196,000.

- There has been a fall in the profit from operations margin of 12.17% (8% + 4.17%).

- This fall is partly due to the fall in the gross profit margin and partly due to an increase in both distribution and administration costs.

- This may not mean that less cash is available to pay debts; it depends on where the profits have gone in the period.

- It is necessary to consider the liquidity of the business and the changes in assets and liabilities.

- There has been an increase in both current assets and liabilities, which may indicate that profits have been tied up in the short-term working capital.

- There has been no investment in non-current assets.

**(d)**   **The interest cover has decreased which means that the company is in a worse position than last year.**

- The interest cover has decreased from 15.05 times to no cover at all.

- The generation of cash is required to pay interest, and the overall cash balance (including overdraft) has fallen by £170,000, which confirms that the company is in a worse position than in the previous year.

**(e)** **The current ratio should be 2 which means that last year it was too high.**

- Referring to the fact that the current ratio should be 2 is a common misunderstanding; the level of an 'acceptable' ratio very much depends on the organisation itself and the type of industry to which it belongs.

- The higher the current ratio the better when carrying out credit assessment.

- The current ratio is a simple measure of solvency and it has fallen significantly in this case from 5.09 to 2.01.

- The component parts of the current assets need to be looked at to determine liquidity.

- The cash balance has been converted to a bank overdraft which is worrying and the trade receivables have increased (see below).

**(f)** **The trade receivables have increased by 50% which supports the conclusion of overtrading.**

- Trade receivables have increased from £619,000 to £928,000 and an increase would be expected with an increase in sales.

- Whether or not this supports overtrading depends on other factors.

- The trade receivables collection period has increased from 60.03 days to 71.99 days. This would indicate that the company is struggling with its credit control procedures and points to overtrading.

**(g)** **The trade payables have increased by £252,000 which indicates the company is not paying its suppliers and requires the increase in the credit limit.**

- Trade payables have increased significantly and the trade payables collection period has increased by 27.92 days.

- The increase is not a good sign, it indicates that the company is struggling to pay its suppliers on time and also points to overtrading.

- This would appear to be the reason why the company has requested an increase in the credit limit and a similar request has possibly been made to other suppliers.

**(h)** **The inventory has remained the same which is a good sign.**

- The inventory levels have remained the same, but with a significant increase in turnover an increase in inventory would usually be expected.

- The inventory holding period has fallen by 22.95 days.

- This may indicate that the business is unable to buy further inventory and inventory may run out.

- Or, it may indicate that the business is handling its inventory levels more efficiently.

**(i)** **The total funding (equity and borrowing) has only increased by £25,000 which is a good sign.**

- The total of equity and borrowing was £1,750,000 and has increased by £25,000 to £1,775,000.

- This is not a good sign because the gearing percentage has increased from 37.14% to 51.21%.

- There has been an increase in both long-term and short-term borrowing and the company is placing a much heavier reliance on borrowing, especially with the introduction of a short-term bank overdraft.

- The bank overdraft and increase in the long-term loan has been used to fund the working capital of the business, as mentioned previously there has been no investment in non-current assets.

(j)    **My conclusion is that credit should be given.**

- Credit should not be given.

- It appears that the company is overtrading and is struggling to pay suppliers on time.

- Long-term and short-term loans have been used to fund the working capital of the business.

# 4    Customer accounts – legal aspects

**4.1**    (b)    Offer, acceptance, consideration, an intention to create legal relations

**4.2**    (d)    The buyer has agreed in principle to all the terms of the contract but the contract has not yet been drawn up

**4.3**    (b)    As described

    (c)    Of satisfactory quality

**4.4**    (b)    'I agree to buy goods from you and will accept your stated terms and conditions'

**4.5**    (a)    John cannot sue Mike because the £1,000 consideration was paid by Magda

**4.6**    (b)    Specific performance

**4.7**    9.5 per cent

**4.8**    £182.47

# 5 Monitoring and controlling customer accounts

**5.1**   Balance @ 31 January 20X3  = £54,276

Balance @ 28 February 20X3  = £35,676

**Note that** the question asks for a calculation of the balances of the account at the end of the two months. This may either be carried out as a straight arithmetic exercise, or it can be done by completing two double-entry accounts as shown below.

| | | £ | | | £ |
|---|---|---|---|---|---|
| 1 Jan | B/fwd | 78,000 | | | |
| 10 Jan | Invoice | 54,000 | 16 Jan | Credit Note | 2,484 |
| | | | 18 Jan | Bank | 75,240 |
| | | | 31 Jan | C/fwd | 54,276 |
| | | 132,000 | | | 132,000 |

| | | £ | | | £ |
|---|---|---|---|---|---|
| 1 Feb | B/fwd | 54,276 | | | |
| 12 Feb | Invoice | 26,400 | 26 Feb | Bank | 45,000 |
| | | | 28 Feb | C/fwd | 35,676 |
| | | 80,676 | | | 80,676 |

**5.2**   **Baritone Ltd**  (a)  Credit Baritone Ltd's account with £50,400 and debit unallocated payments with £50,400

**Bass Ltd**  (d)  A statement should have been sent on 29 August 20X3

**Contralto Ltd**  (c)  Contact the insolvency practitioner and register a claim with the credit insurer

**Soprano Ltd**   Contact the credit insurer to make a claim for **£11,600**, make a provision for **£2,900** and claim VAT of **£2,900** from HMRC.

**Tenor Ltd**  (c)  Send a copy of the signed delivery note which was signed by Tenor Ltd

**5.3**   (b)   Late Payment of Commercial Debts (Interest) Act

**5.4**   (a)   A credit insurance company

**5.5**   **61** days.

| **6** | **Collecting debts and dealing with insolvency** |
|---|---|

**6.1**    (c)    Multi Track

**6.2**    (b)    An order which will authorise an employer to deduct regular amounts from the customer's salary in order to repay the debt

**6.3**    (b)    £750

**6.4**    (a)    The goods can be identified as having been supplied by the seller, for example with a stamp or label

**6.5**    **(1)**    The dividend (pence per £1) payable to the trade payables:    60p

      **(2)**    The amount that will be received by Lewis Enterprises:    £6,000

      **(3)**    The amount that will be written off as an irrecoverable debt:    £4,000

**Workings:**

**(1)**    £150K available for trade payables (£500K − £350K) ÷ £250K =  60p

**(2)**    Dividend to Lewis Enterprises £10,000 x 60p = £6,000

**(3)**    £4,000 (£10K balance − £6K dividend paid)

# Practice assessment 1

**Task 1**

**(a)** An offer in relation to a contract of sale can be made:

✔

| | | |
|---|---|---|
| (a) | Only by the seller | |
| (b) | Only by the buyer | |
| (c) | By the buyer or by the seller | . |

Tick the **one** correct option.

**(b)** All valid contracts contain the following four elements:

✔

| | | |
|---|---|---|
| (a) | Offer, acceptance, consideration, guarantee | |
| (b) | Offer, acceptance, consideration, an invitation to treat | |
| (c) | Offer, acceptance, consideration, an intention to create legal relations | |

Tick the **one** correct option.

**(c)** The Sale of Goods Act states that goods sold must be:

✔

| | | |
|---|---|---|
| (a) | Of satisfactory quality | |
| (b) | Of acceptable quality | |
| (c) | Fit for the purpose | |
| (d) | Guaranteed for 12 months | |

Tick the **two** correct options.

**(d)**    A shop has set up a notice board where customers can advertise goods and services for sale to the public. These adverts constitute in contract:

✔

| (a) | An offer | |
|-----|----------|---|
| (b) | Terms and conditions | |
| (c) | An invitation to treat | |

Tick the **one** correct option.

**(e)**    Bella decides that she wants to sell her car, a classic Porsche for £40,000. She puts a notice quoting this price in a specialist magazine. She receives an email from an enthusiastic buyer offering her £39,500 for the car. In contract this email is:

✔

| (a) | An acceptance | |
|-----|---------------|---|
| (b) | Consideration | |
| (c) | An offer | |

Tick the **one** correct option.

**(f)**    A breach of contract occurs when:    ✔

| (a) | The contract has not been signed | |
|-----|----------------------------------|---|
| (b) | The contract is signed by a person not authorised to sign it | |
| (c) | The terms of the contract are not fulfilled | |

Tick the **one** correct option.

**(g)**   The Late Payments of Commercial Debts (Interest) Act allows small companies to charge interest to customers who exceed their credit terms and pay late. The interest charge is based on the current bank base rate.

**You are to** enter in the box below the percentage rate charged.

If the current base rate is 0.5%, the late payment interest rate is ⬚ per cent.

**(h)**   A customer owes £5,000 (excluding VAT @ 20%) and the debt is 45 days late.

**You are to** calculate the interest charge under the Late Payments of Commercial Debts (Interest) Act to the nearest penny. Enter the figure in the box below. The bank base rate is 2%.

£ ⬚

**(i)**   **You are to** enter each of the following words into the correct box within the text which follows.

**individuals**          **companies**          **manual**          **principles**

The Data Protection Act protects data held about ⬚ and not

⬚ . It covers both computer-based and ⬚

records. It is based around eight guiding ⬚ which protect the data held.

**Task 2**

**(a)**   Which **one** of the following options is the most useful source of information about a customer's ability to pay invoices on time?

✔

| | | |
|---|---|---|
| (a) | The customer's Statement of Profit or Loss | |
| (b) | A credit rating agency | |
| (c) | Official publications | |

Tick the correct option.

**(b)**   Efficient day-to-day collection by a business of money owed by customers  is best achieved through:

✔

| | | |
|---|---|---|
| (a) | The use of an outside debt collection agency | |
| (b) | A clearly set out and comprehensive credit control policy | |
| (c) | The use of the Small Claims procedure | |

Tick **one** option.

**(c)**   A small business has a £7,000 debt outstanding on a customer account. Despite all its efforts, including a solicitor's letter, the business is unable to recover the money. Through which Court process should this claim be pursued?

✔

| | | |
|---|---|---|
| (a) | Multi Track | |
| (b) | Fast Track | |
| (c) | Small Claims Track | |

Tick the **one** appropriate option.

**(d)** A garnishee order is:

|  |  | ✔ |
|---|---|---|
| (a) | A court order sent to a third party such as a bank which has an account for the customer requiring the money to be paid direct to the seller | |
| (b) | An order for the court bailiffs to enter the property of the customer who owes money to the seller to seize valuable assets | |
| (c) | An order which will give the seller a right to the sale proceeds of property owned by the customer | |

Tick the **one** correct option.

**(e)** An understanding of insolvency involves the use of very specific terminology. The term 'liquidation' is used in relation to:

|  |  | ✔ |
|---|---|---|
| (a) | A sole trader | |
| (b) | A limited company | |
| (c) | An unincorporated partnership | |

Tick the **one** correct option.

**(f)** A statutory demand made on a trade receivable for an outstanding debt should be for a minimum of:

|  |  | ✔ |
|---|---|---|
| (a) | £750 | |
| (b) | £1,000 | |
| (c) | £10,000 | |

Tick the **one** correct option.

**(g)**    Administration as it relates to insolvency can be defined as:

|  |  |  | ✔ |
|---|---|---|---|
| (a) | The situation where a company having solvency problems is placed in the hands of an Administrator appointed by the court; the Administration process helps to protect the business and will try to return it to solvency | | |
| (b) | The situation where a bank that has a floating charge over the assets of a company can appoint an Administrative Receiver who is authorised to sell the secured assets of the company in order to repay the bank borrowing | | |
| (c) | The situation where a court makes an order authorising bailiffs to obtain and sell off the assets owned by a business which refuses to pay its trade debts | | |

Tick the **one** correct option.

**(h)**    Pargetter Ltd's standard credit terms of payment are 30 days. It offers to customers an early settlement discount of 1.5% for payment within 15 days of invoice.

The simple annual interest rate of the discount is: ⬜ per cent.

Calculations should be to two decimal places.

**(i)**    Green Ltd is a regular customer of Geller Ltd. During the year Green Ltd bought from Geller Ltd 650 items which cost £250 each, including VAT at 20%. At the end of the year Green Ltd's balance of account was £13,500.

The receivables collection period (to the nearest day) is: ⬜ days.

**Task 3**

You work as a Credit Control Manager for Lawson Ltd which uses a credit rating system to assess the credit status of new customers. The credit rating (scoring) system is used to assess the risk of default by calculating key indicators (ratios), comparing them to the table and calculating an aggregate score. This system is set out below.

| Credit rating (scoring) system | Score |
| --- | --- |
| **Profit from operations margin** | |
| Losses | −5 |
| Less than 5% | 0 |
| 5% and above but less than 10% | 5 |
| 10% and above but less than 20% | 10 |
| 20% or more | 20 |
| **Interest cover** | |
| No cover | −30 |
| Less than 1 | −20 |
| 1 and above but less than 2 | −10 |
| 2 and above but less than 4 | 0 |
| 4 or more | 10 |
| **Liquidity ratio – quick ratio** | |
| Less than 1 | −20 |
| 1 and above but less than 1.25 | −10 |
| 1.25 and above but less than 1.5 | 0 |
| 1.5 or more | 10 |
| **Gearing (total debt / total debt plus equity)** | |
| Less than 25% | 20 |
| 25% and above but less than 50% | 10 |
| 50% and above but less than 65% | 0 |
| 65% and above but less than 75% | −20 |
| 75% and above but less than 80% | −40 |
| 80% or more | −100 |

| Risk | Aggregate score |
|------|-----------------|
| Very low risk | Between 60 and 21 |
| Low risk | Between 20 and 1 |
| Medium risk | Between 0 and −24 |
| High risk | Between −25 and −50 |
| Very high risk | Between −50 and −160 |

The Sales Department has asked for a credit limit of £45,000 to be given to Sunny Limited, a potential new customer. The financial information below has been supplied by Sunny Limited.

**Sunny Limited: Statement of Profit or Loss**

|  | 20X3 | 20X2 |
|--|------|------|
|  | *£000* | *£000* |
| Sales revenue | 4,200 | 3,850 |
| Cost of sales | 2,495 | 2,329 |
| Gross profit | 1,705 | 1,521 |
| Distribution costs | 206 | 147 |
| Administration expenses | 869 | 604 |
| Profit from operations | 630 | 770 |
| Finance costs | 36 | 77 |
| Profit before taxation | 594 | 693 |
| Taxation | 120 | 150 |
| Profit for the year | 474 | 543 |

**Sunny Limited: Statement of Financial Position**

|  | 20X3 | 20X2 |
|---|---|---|
|  | *£000* | *£000* |
| **ASSETS** |  |  |
| **Non-current assets** |  |  |
| Property, plant and equipment | 1,832 | 1,846 |
|  |  |  |
| **Current assets** |  |  |
| Inventories | 68 | 54 |
| Trade and other receivables | 450 | 650 |
| Cash | 1,350 | 1,450 |
|  | 1,868 | 2,154 |
| **Total assets** | 3,700 | 4,000 |
|  |  |  |
| **EQUITY AND LIABILITIES** |  |  |
| **Equity** |  |  |
| Share capital | 1,200 | 1,000 |
| Retained earnings | 525 | 450 |
| **Total equity** | 1,725 | 1,450 |
|  |  |  |
| **Non-current liabilities** |  |  |
| Borrowing | 850 | 1,050 |
| **Current liabilities** |  |  |
| Borrowings | 380 | 505 |
| Trade and other payables | 745 | 995 |
| **Total liabilities** | 1,975 | 2,550 |
| **Total equity and liabilities** | 3,700 | 4,000 |

**(a)** Complete the table below by calculating the key indicators (to 2 decimal places) for 20X3 and 20X2 for Sunny Limited, and rate the company using the credit rating scoring system.

| Sunny Limited | 20X3 Indicator | 20X3 Rating | 20X2 Indicator | 20X2 Rating |
|---|---|---|---|---|
| Profit from operations margin % | | | | |
| Interest cover | | | | |
| Quick ratio | | | | |
| Gearing % | | | | |
| Total credit rating | | | | |

**(b)** Based on the results of your credit rating and using the table below, recommend whether the requested credit limit should be given to Sunny Limited.

| Rating | Decision |
|---|---|
| Very low or low risk current year and very low or low risk previous year | Accept |
| Very low or low risk current year and medium risk previous year | Accept |
| Very low or low risk current year and high or very high risk previous year | Request latest management accounts and defer decision |
| Very high risk or high risk current year | Reject |
| Medium risk current year and medium, low or very low risk previous year | Accept |
| Medium risk current year and high or very high risk previous year | Request latest management accounts and defer decision |

✔

| Credit decision | |
|---|---|
| (a) Accept | |
| (b) Reject | |
| (c) Request latest management accounts and defer decision | |

**Task 4**

The Sales Department has asked for a credit limit of £18,500 to be given to Howard Limited, a potential new customer. The financial information on this and the next page has been supplied by Howard Limited.

**Howard Limited: Statement of Profit or Loss**

|  | 20X2 | 20X1 |
|---|---|---|
|  | *£000* | *£000* |
| Sales revenue | 1,750 | 2,100 |
| Cost of sales | 1,083 | 1,242 |
| Gross profit | 667 | 858 |
| Distribution costs | 53 | 59 |
| Administration expenses | 779 | 748 |
| Profit (loss) from operations | (165) | 51 |
| Finance costs | 11 | 8 |
| Profit / (loss) before taxation | (176) | 43 |
| Taxation | - | 10 |
| Profit / (loss) for the year | (176) | 33 |

**Howard Limited: Statement of Financial Position**

|  | 20X2 | 20X1 |
|---|---|---|
|  | *£000* | *£000* |
| **ASSETS** |  |  |
| **Non-current assets** |  |  |
| Property, plant and equipment | 771 | 613 |
|  |  |  |
| **Current assets** |  |  |
| Inventories | 116 | 112 |
| Trade and other receivables | 147 | 268 |
| Cash | 5 | 11 |
|  | 268 | 391 |
| **Total assets** | 1,039 | 1,004 |
|  |  |  |
| **EQUITY AND LIABILITIES** |  |  |
| **Equity** |  |  |
| Share capital | 400 | 350 |
| Retained earnings | 158 | 334 |
| **Total equity** | 558 | 684 |
|  |  |  |
| **Non-current liabilities** |  |  |
| Borrowing | 250 | 150 |
|  |  |  |
| **Current liabilities** |  |  |
| Borrowings | 17 | - |
| Trade and other payables | 214 | 170 |
| **Total liabilities** | 481 | 320 |
| **Total equity and liabilities** | 1,039 | 1,004 |

**(a)**    Complete the table below by calculating the key indicators (to 2 decimal places) for 20X2 and 20X1 for Howard Limited.

| Howard Limited | 20X2 Indicator | 20X1 Indicator |
|---|---|---|
| Gross profit margin % | | |
| Profit from operations margin % | | |
| Trade payables payment period in days | | |
| Inventory holding period in days | | |
| Current ratio | | |
| Quick ratio | | |

**(b)** You have been asked to prepare some points to include in an email to the Chief Credit Controller to assist in his decision whether to give credit to Howard Ltd.

Refer to Howard Ltd's financial statements and the key performance indicators calculated in (a) and complete the points detailed below by inserting the appropriate figure or selecting the correct option.

(1) Sales revenue for 20X2 compared to 20X1 has decreased by ☐ %

which means that the company may have

**sold fewer units / increased the unit selling price / experienced an increased demand for its products.**

(2) The gross profit margin has **increased / decreased**, which means that the company has

**increased the selling price / increased the purchase price / left both the selling and purchase price of its products unchanged.**

(3) At operational level the company is making a **profit / loss** which

**is not a problem as cash not profit pays liabilities / may be a problem depending on the cash flow of the business / is a problem as profits are needed to pay liabilities / is not a problem as gross profit is sufficient to pay liabilities.**

(4) The current ratio measures **short-term solvency / short-term insolvency / long-term solvency** of an organisation. In this case it has **increased / decreased** and is **less than 1 / still greater than 1**, which is **a sign of insolvency / a sign of poor liquidity / a good sign**.

(5) The quick ratio has **risen / fallen** to ☐ which **is / is not** a major concern in terms of liquidity.

(6) The inventory holding period has **increased / decreased**. This may mean that inventory **is slow moving / could run out / levels are too low.**

(7) The trade payables payment period has **increased / decreased** by ☐

days. This may indicate that the company has **sufficient / insufficient** liquidity and is **likely / unlikely** to pays its liabilities as they fall due.

(8) On the basis of the financial statements that have been provided to us and the key performance indicators I recommend that **credit be given / credit not be given** to Howard Ltd.

**Task 5**

James Limited has been trading with Lawson Limited for several years and has, until recently, always complied with its credit terms. Following several late payments James Limited contacted Lawson Limited to request an increase in its credit limit from £30,000 to £60,000. James Limited has supplied the Statement of Profit or Loss (below) and the Statement of Financial Position (on the next page.)

**James Limited: Statement of Profit or Loss**

|  | 20X2 | 20X1 |
|---|---|---|
|  | £000 | £000 |
| Sales revenue | 5,988 | 4,785 |
| Cost of sales | 3,293 | 2,631 |
| Gross profit | 2,695 | 2,154 |
| Distribution costs | 370 | 289 |
| Administration expenses | 1,966 | 1,969 |
| Profit / (loss) from operations | 359 | (104) |
| Finance costs | 45 | 110 |
| Profit / (loss) before taxation | 314 | (214) |
| Taxation | 45 | - |
| Profit / (loss) for the year | 269 | (214) |

**James Limited: Statement of Financial Position**

|  | 20X2 | 20X1 |
|---|---|---|
|  | £000 | £000 |
| **ASSETS** |  |  |
| **Non-current assets** |  |  |
| Property, plant and equipment | 1,491 | 1,485 |
|  |  |  |
| **Current assets** |  |  |
| Inventories | 370 | 296 |
| Trade and other receivables | 1,202 | 1,115 |
| Cash | 167 | - |
|  | 1,739 | 1,411 |
| **Total assets** | 3,230 | 2,896 |
|  |  |  |
| **EQUITY AND LIABILITIES** |  |  |
| **Equity** |  |  |
| Share capital | 750 | 500 |
| Retained earnings | 950 | 700 |
| **Total equity** | 1,700 | 1,200 |
|  |  |  |
| **Non-current liabilities** |  |  |
| Borrowing | 1,050 | 500 |
|  |  |  |
| **Current liabilities** |  |  |
| Bank overdraft | - | 800 |
| Trade and other payables | 480 | 396 |
| **Total liabilities** | 1,530 | 1,696 |
| **Total equity and liabilities** | 3,230 | 2,896 |

The credit analysis team at Lawson Limited has calculated financial indicators from the financial statements provided by James Limited.

These indicators are shown at the top of the next page.

| James Limited | 20X2 | 20X1 |
|---|---|---|
| Gross profit margin % | 45.01 | 45.02 |
| Profit from operations margin % | 6.00 | −2.17 |
| Interest cover | 7.98 | none |
| Current ratio | 3.62 | 1.18 |
| Trade payables payment period in days | 53.2 | 54.94 |
| Trade receivables collection period in days | 73.27 | 85.05 |
| Inventory holding period in days | 41.01 | 41.06 |
| Gearing % | 38.18 | 52.00 |

The Sales Manager of Lawson Limited has reviewed the financial statements provided by James Limited and the financial indicators shown above and has made comments suggesting that credit should not be given to James Limited. These comments are set out below.

1. The company's turnover has increased by 25.14% from £4,785,000 to £5,988,000. This is a strong sign of overtrading.

2. The profit from operations has increased by £359,000. This means that more cash is available to pay debts.

3. The interest cover has increased which means that the company is in a worse position than last year.

4. The current ratio should be 2 which means that last year the company was insolvent, but this year the company is solvent.

5. The trade receivables have increased by 92.76% which supports the conclusion of overtrading.

6. The trade payables have increased by £84,000 which indicates the company is not paying its suppliers.

7. The inventory has increased by £74,000 which supports the conclusion of overtrading.

8. Gearing has decreased which means that the banks are not happy to lend money to the business.

(a)    **You are to** write brief bullet point notes dealing with the accuracy and validity of each comment that the Sales Manager has made.

Use the data available to you in the financial statements and table of financial indicators to support your comments.

**(b)**    **You are to** state whether or not you would recommend granting the increase in credit limit to James Limited:

| | ✔ |
|---|---|
| Yes | |
| No | |

**Task 6**

You have been provided with the credit control policy for William Limited. Today's date is 31 May 20X3.

The company's credit control procedures are as follows:

1. An order for goods is received by email, fax or phone (all phone calls are recorded).

2. Goods are delivered and a goods received note is signed by the customer.

3. The goods received notes are kept in a file in the accounts office.

4. An invoice will be issued on the day after delivery on 30 day terms.

5. An aged analysis of trade receivables is produced weekly.

6. A reminder telephone call is made when the debt is 7 days overdue.

7. When a debt is 14 days overdue a letter is sent.

8. When a debt is 28 days overdue the account will be put on stop.

9. The debt will either be placed in the hands of a debt collection company or legal proceedings could be instigated if the customer does not respond to calls or letters.

10. The business is credit insured, but insurance cover is only for customers once they have a history of trade with the business of at least 12 months and have successfully paid for at least three invoiced amounts. Only 80% of the value of the debt is insured. VAT will be reclaimed from HMRC.

The assistant responsible for credit control has been on maternity leave for several months but you have access to the notes she has prepared.

**You are to** identify the most appropriate course of action for each customer based on the information provided.

**(a)    Bronson Ltd**

The balance on Bronson Ltd's account is £22,560. This consists of two invoices, one for £12,960 which is not overdue and one for £9,600 which is overdue. An unallocated payment has been received for £9,600 and posted to the unallocated payment accounts in the purchase ledger. It has now been identified as a receipt from Bronson Ltd.

The action needed is to:

✔

| | |
|---|---|
| (a) Credit Bronson Ltd's account with £9,600 and debit unallocated payments with £9,600 | |
| (b) Debit Bronson Ltd's account with £9,600 and debit unallocated payments with £9,600 | |
| (c) Credit Bronson Ltd's account with £9,600 and credit unallocated payments with £9,600 | |
| (d) Debit Bronson Ltd's account with £9,600 and credit unallocated payments with £9,600 | |

**(b)    Rednap Ltd**

This new customer placed its first order a few weeks ago. The goods were delivered on 1 May 20X3 and the invoice was issued on 10 May 20X3 on 30 day terms.

The action needed is:

|  |  | ✔ |
|---|---|---|
| (a) | The account should be put on stop | |
| (b) | The account is not overdue so no action is required | |
| (c) | Rednap Ltd should be contacted and an immediate payment requested | |
| (d) | A phone call should have been made on 17 May 20X3 and a letter sent on 24 May 20X3 | |

**(c)    Hathaway Ltd**

A balance of £17,400 is 68 days overdue and is for one invoice. Hathaway Ltd claims that the goods were not received.

The action needed is to:

|  |  | ✔ |
|---|---|---|
| (a) | Send the original delivery note signed by Hathaway Ltd | |
| (b) | Raise a credit note for £17,400 | |
| (c) | Send a copy of the signed delivery note which was signed by Hathaway Ltd | |
| (d) | Send a copy of the signed delivery note signed by the courier who delivered the package | |

**(d)    Winslet Ltd**

Winslet Ltd sent a payment of £11,400 but did not provide details of the invoices to which the payment relates.

The action needed is:

|  |  | ✔ |
|---|---|---|
| (a) | Winslet Ltd should be contacted to confirm which invoices are being paid so that the unallocated receipt can be allocated | |
| (b) | The £11,400 should be returned to Winslet Ltd | |
| (c) | The £11,400 should be allocated to the last invoice first | |
| (d) | The £11,400 should be posted to unallocated payments | |

**(e)** **Klunee Ltd**

Klunee Ltd owes a balance of £42,720 including VAT. The account is on stop. Attempts to contact the customer by telephone have been unsuccessful. The account is credit insured.

Complete the sentence below:

Contact the credit insurer to make a claim for £ [_____], make a provision for

£ [_____] and claim VAT of £ [_____] from HMRC.

**(f)** **Taylor Ltd**

Taylor Ltd has gone into administration after being a customer for five years. Up until six months ago, the company had always complied with its credit terms.

The action needed is to:

|  |  | ✔ |
|---|---|---|
| (a) | Place the account on stop and contact a debt collection company to deal with processing a claim against Taylor Ltd | |
| (b) | Contact the insolvency service and register a claim with the credit insurer | |
| (c) | Visit the premises of Taylor Ltd and seize goods to the value of the outstanding balance | |
| (d) | Contact the insolvency practitioner and register a claim with the credit insurer | |

**Task 7**

Snowden Ltd supplies goods to the manufacturing sector. The standard terms and conditions printed on the back of every sales invoice raised by Snowden Ltd include a retention of title clause and also a requirement that problems with goods must be notified to Snowden Ltd within 24 hours of delivery. Goods returned are subject to a restocking fee of 10%.

You work in the Credit Control Department and the date is 30 September 20X3, the company's financial year-end.

The Senior Credit Controller is ill but has left you a copy of the company's credit control policy together with notes on some of the customer accounts. An extract of these notes is provided below:

---

**Credit control procedures**

1.   An order for goods is received by email, fax or phone (all phone calls are recorded).

2.   Goods are delivered and a goods received note is signed by the customer.

3.   The goods received notes are kept in a file in the accounts office.

4.   An invoice will be issued on the day after delivery on 30 day terms.

5.   An aged analysis of trade receivables is produced weekly.

6.   A reminder telephone call is made when the debt is 7 days overdue.

7.   When a debt is 14 days overdue a letter is sent.

8.   When a debt is 28 days overdue the account will be put on stop.

9.   The debt will either be placed in the hands of a debt collection company or legal proceedings could be instigated if the customer does not respond to calls or letters.

10.   The business is credit insured, however insurance is only given for customers once they have a history of trade with the business of at least 12 months and have successfully paid for at least three invoiced amounts. Only 70% of the value of the debt is insured.

11.   All sales invoices include VAT at the standard rate of 20% and VAT is recovered from HMRC under its Bad Debt Relief Scheme where applicable.

---

**(a)**   Review the information provided for each of three customers of Snowden Ltd on the next two pages and prepare a list of actions for collecting the outstanding amounts due to Snowden Ltd.

Your list of actions should include a summary of the options available for the company to pursue and recommendations for provisions or write-off of irrecoverable debts where appropriate.

### Downside Ltd

The sales ledger of Snowden Ltd shows a balance outstanding of £67,200 which relates to one invoice dated 31 August 20X3. You have seen in the local papers that Downside Ltd went into administration on 14 September 20X3.

### Whistle Ltd

Whistle Ltd has gone into liquidation owing Snowden Ltd £5,400 (including VAT) for a debt which is over 6 months old. Snowden Ltd has contacted the liquidator who has stated that it is unlikely that the retention of title will be valid because Whistle Ltd purchased similar items from several suppliers and therefore the goods are not identified as being supplied by Snowden Ltd.

**Vanilla Ltd**

Vanilla Ltd are refusing to pay an invoice of £9,600 from June 20X3 claiming that the goods were not ordered. They are requesting that Snowden Ltd collect the goods. Vanilla Ltd has been a customer for many years and normally pays promptly; all subsequent invoices have been paid in full. There is no record of the order; however, the goods received note was signed by Vanilla Ltd.

You also have to deal with two further customers, Mountain Limited and Chute Limited.

**(b)**    **Mountain Ltd**

The sales ledger account for Mountain Ltd has become corrupted but the following information is available:

- Balance 1 August 20X3 - £45,000

- Invoices raised: 2 August 20X3 £10,000 plus VAT at 20%, 24 September 20X3 £3,840 (VAT inclusive)

- Credit notes raised: 6 August 20X3 £1,200 (VAT inclusive) subject to a restocking fee of 10%

- Bank receipts: 16 August 20X3 £45,000, 16 September 20X3 £10,000

**You are to** calculate the balances on the account of Mountain Ltd at 31 August 20X3 and 30 September 20X3.

**(c)** **Chute Ltd**

No action has been taken in respect of the account for Chute Ltd, who have an agreed credit limit of £30,000. The account transactions are listed below, and today's date is 30 June 20X3:

- Invoice of £30,000 plus VAT at 20% on 15 March 20X3

- Invoice of £24,000 plus VAT at 20% on 5 May 20X3

Identify the actions, with dates, that should have been undertaken by the credit control team at Snowden Ltd:

# Practice assessment 2

**Task 1**

**(a)** An offer in relation to a contract of sale may be terminated in the following **two** circumstances:

✔

| | | |
|---|---|---|
| (a) | When a time limit fixed for acceptance has expired | |
| (b) | If the buyer decides to back out of the contract after it has been agreed | |
| (c) | By the buyer making a counter offer | |

Tick the **two** correct options.

**(b)** 'The intention to create legal relations' as it relates to contract means that:

✔

| | | |
|---|---|---|
| (a) | The agreement can be enforced in a court of law if necessary | |
| (b) | The contract will need to be approved by a solicitor | |
| (c) | A contract can be a domestic arrangement between relations | |

Tick the **one** correct option.

**(c)** The Unfair Contract Terms Act gives protection to the purchaser of goods and services: ✔

| | | |
|---|---|---|
| (a) | When there are conditions in the small print of a contract which the purchaser does not understand | |
| (b) | When there are conditions in the small print of a contract which a court of law would find unreasonable | |
| (c) | When the contract is part of a fraud or illegal scam | |

Tick the **one** correct option.

**(d)**    An online bookshop offers for sale a new book 'Credit Control in a Nutshell' with the offer of a 20% discount for the first month. This constitutes in contract:    ✔

| | | |
|---|---|---|
| (a) | An offer | |
| (b) | An invitation to treat | |
| (c) | Consideration | |

Tick the **one** correct option.

**(e)**    Leroy wants to sell his motor bike for £25,000. He puts a notice in the paper advertising the price but nobody replies. He says to a friend 'You can buy this motor bike at a knock-down price of £20,000. If I don't hear from you within one week I will consider the deal is done.'

In this case his friend has provided:    ✔

| | | |
|---|---|---|
| (a) | An acceptance | |
| (b) | No acceptance | |
| (c) | A counter offer | |

Tick the **one** correct option.

**(f)**    'Action for the price' means:    ✔

| | | |
|---|---|---|
| (a) | Taking legal action in the courts for recovery of an unpaid debt | |
| (b) | Increasing the price of goods beyond the contracted amount | |
| (c) | Effective communication of the price of goods to the buyer | |

Tick the **one** correct option.

**(g)** The Late Payments of Commercial Debts (Interest) Act allows small companies to charge interest to customers who exceed their credit terms and pay late. The interest charge is based on the current bank base rate.

**You are to** enter in the box below the percentage rate charged.

If the current base rate is 1%, the late payment interest rate is [        ] per cent.

**(h)** A customer owes £6,000 (excluding VAT @ 20%) and the debt is 50 days late.

**You are to** calculate the interest charge under the Late Payments of Commercial Debts (Interest) Act to the nearest penny. Enter the figure in the box below. The bank base rate is 1.75%.

£ [        ]

**(i)** **You are to** enter each of the following phrases into the correct box within the text which follows.

**hire purchase agreements**          **granting of credit**          **credit sale agreements**

The Consumer Credit Act regulates most agreements for the [        ] .

These include [        ] where ownership passes to the

purchaser straightaway on purchase and also [        ]

where the consumer pays instalments to hire the item but will only take ownership when the final

instalment has been paid.

**Task 2**

**(a)**    Your business is assessing the credit status of a new customer who has applied for credit terms. Which **one** of the following options is the most useful source of information about the customer's ability to pay invoices on time?

| | | ✔ |
|---|---|---|
| (a) | A search at Companies House for the customer's filed accounts | |
| (b) | A trade receivables analysis | |
| (c) | Supplier trade references | |

Tick the appropriate option.

**(b)**    A business wanting to employ an independent company to help with the running of its Sales Ledger and the issue of invoices is most likely to use the following service:

| | | ✔ |
|---|---|---|
| (a) | Factoring | |
| (b) | Invoice discounting | |
| (c) | Credit insurance | |

Tick the appropriate option.

**(c)**    A business has a £2,000 debt outstanding on a customer account. One of the excuses made by the customer for non-payment is that it had not issued a Purchase Order and the seller had consequently sent the wrong goods. Given these circumstances, what is the remedy (if any) that the seller should pursue?

| | | ✔ |
|---|---|---|
| (a) | A County Court action for the amount owed for the goods supplied | |
| (b) | A Statutory Demand for the amount owed for the goods supplied | |
| (c) | As there was no defined offer or acceptance there is unlikely to be a contract and so no remedies are likely to succeed | |

Tick the appropriate option.

**(d)** A warrant of execution is:

| | | ✔ |
|---|---|---|
| (a) | A court order sent to a third party such as a bank which has an account for the customer requiring the money to be paid direct to the seller | |
| (b) | An order for the court bailiffs to seize assets belonging to a customer who owes money to the seller | |
| (c) | An order which will authorise an employer to deduct regular amounts from the customer's salary in order to repay the debt | |

Tick the **one** correct option.

**(e)** An understanding of insolvency involves the use of very specific terminology. The term 'bankruptcy' is used in relation to:

| | | ✔ |
|---|---|---|
| (a) | A sole trader | |
| (b) | A private limited company | |
| (c) | A public limited company | |

Tick the **one** correct option.

**(f)** A statutory demand made on a trade receivable for an outstanding debt should be for a minimum of:

| | | ✔ |
|---|---|---|
| (a) | £5,000 | |
| (b) | £1,000 | |
| (c) | £750 | |

Tick the **one** correct option.

**(g)**   An Administrative Receiver is an insolvency practitioner who is:

| | | | ✔ |
|---|---|---|---|
| (a) | Appointed by the court in the situation where a company is having solvency problems and the court considers the Administrative Receiver has a reasonable chance of being able to rescue the company | | |
| (b) | Appointed by a bank under its floating charge and is authorised to sell the secured assets of the company in order to repay the bank borrowing in preference to unsecured trade payables | | |
| (c) | Appointed by the court in a company liquidation and has the task of calculating how much goes to each payable when the company assets are sold | | |

Tick the **one** correct option.

**(h)**   Carter Ltd's standard credit terms of payment are 60 days. It offers to customers an early settlement discount of 2% for payment within 30 days of invoice.

The simple annual interest rate of the discount is: [        ]  per cent.

Calculations should be to two decimal places.

**(i)**   Buffay Ltd is a regular customer of Hartmann Ltd. During the year Buffay Ltd bought from Hartmann Ltd 2,200 items which cost £95 each, including VAT at 20%. At the end of the year Buffay Ltd's balance of account was £21,600.

The receivables collection period (to the nearest day) is: [        ]  days.

**Task 3**

You work in the finance section of Standard Services Ltd which uses a credit rating system to assess the credit status of new and existing customers. Part of your role is to use the credit rating (scoring) system to assess the risk of default by calculating key indicators (ratios), comparing them to the table and calculating an aggregate score. This system is set out below.

| Credit rating (scoring ) system | Score |
|---|---|
| **Profit from operations margin** | |
| Losses | −5 |
| Less than 5% | 0 |
| 5% and above but less than 10% | 5 |
| 10% and above but less than 20% | 10 |
| 20% or more | 20 |
| **Interest cover** | |
| No cover | −30 |
| Less than 1 | −20 |
| 1 and above but less than 2 | −10 |
| 2 and above but less than 4 | 0 |
| 4 or more | 10 |
| **Liquidity ratio** | |
| Less than 1 | −20 |
| 1 and above but less than 1.25 | −10 |
| 1.25 and above but less than 1.5 | 0 |
| 1.5 or more | 10 |
| **Gearing (total debt / total debt plus equity)** | |
| Less than 25% | 20 |
| 25% and above but less than 50% | 10 |
| 50% and above but less than 65% | 0 |
| 65% and above but less than 75% | −20 |
| 75% and above but less than 80% | −40 |
| 80% or more | −100 |

| Risk | Aggregate score |
|---|---|
| Very low risk | Between 60 and 21 |
| Low risk | Between 20 and 1 |
| Medium risk | Between 0 and −24 |
| High risk | Between −25 and −50 |
| Very high risk | Between −50 and −160 |

The Sales Department has asked for a credit limit of £16,000 to be given to SKP Limited, a potential new customer. The financial statements on this and the next page have been supplied by SKP Limited.

**SKP Limited: Statement of Profit or Loss**

| | 20X2 | 20X1 |
|---|---|---|
| | £ | £ |
| Sales revenue | 1,565,000 | 1,784,000 |
| Cost of sales | 1,181,575 | 1,202,416 |
| Gross profit | 383,425 | 581,584 |
| Distribution costs | 40,784 | 35,266 |
| Administration expenses | 593,041 | 474,958 |
| Profit / (loss) from operations | (250,400) | 71,360 |
| Finance costs | 12,520 | 11,150 |
| Profit / (loss) before taxation | (262,920) | 60,210 |
| Taxation | - | 12,000 |
| Profit / (loss) for the year | (262,920) | 48,210 |

**SKP Limited: Statement of Financial Position**

|  | 20X2 | 20X1 |
|---|---|---|
|  | £ | £ |
| **ASSETS** |  |  |
| **Non-current assets** |  |  |
| Property, plant and equipment | 497,755 | 658,625 |
|  |  |  |
| **Current assets** |  |  |
| Inventories | 150,625 | 73,500 |
| Trade and other receivables | 235,000 | 181,000 |
| Cash | 1,450 | 19,625 |
|  | 387,075 | 274,125 |
| **Total assets** | 884,830 | 932,750 |
|  |  |  |
| **EQUITY AND LIABILITIES** |  |  |
| **Equity** |  |  |
| Share capital | 100,000 | 100,000 |
| Retained earnings | 37,080 | 300,000 |
| **Total equity** | 137,080 | 400,000 |
|  |  |  |
| **Non-current liabilities** |  |  |
| Borrowing | 450,000 | 350,000 |
|  |  |  |
| **Current liabilities** |  |  |
| Trade and other payables | 297,750 | 182,750 |
| **Total liabilities** | 747,750 | 532,750 |
| **Total equity and liabilities** | 884,830 | 932,750 |

**(a)** Complete the table below by calculating the key indicators (to 2 decimal places) for 20X2 and 20X1 for SKP Limited, and rate the company using the credit rating scoring system.

| SKP Limited | 20X2 Indicator | 20X2 Rating | 20X1 Indicator | 20X1 Rating |
|---|---|---|---|---|
| Profit from operations margin % | | | | |
| Interest cover | | | | |
| Current ratio | | | | |
| Gearing % | | | | |
| Total credit rating | | | | |

**(b)** Based on the results of your credit rating and using the table below, recommend whether the requested credit limit should be given to SKP Limited.

| Rating | Decision |
|---|---|
| Very low or low risk current year and very low or low risk previous year | Accept |
| Very low or low risk current year and medium risk previous year | Accept |
| Very low or low risk current year and high or very high risk previous year | Request latest management accounts and defer decision |
| Very high risk or high risk current year | Reject |
| Medium risk current year and medium, low or very low risk previous year | Accept |
| Medium risk current year and high or very high risk previous year | Request latest management accounts and defer decision |

✔

| **Credit decision** | |
|---|---|
| (a)      Accept | |
| (b)      Reject | |
| (c)      Request latest management accounts and defer decision | |

**Task 4**

The Sales Department has asked for a credit limit of £34,000 to be given to Weber Limited who is a potential new customer. The financial information below has been supplied by Weber Limited.

**Weber Limited: Statement of Profit or Loss**

|  | 20X4 | 20X3 |
|---|---|---|
|  | *£000* | *£000* |
| Sales revenue | 3,988 | 3,560 |
| Cost of sales | 1,557 | 1,424 |
| Gross profit | 2,431 | 2,136 |
| Distribution costs | 79 | 63 |
| Administration expenses | 1,485 | 1,352 |
| Profit from operations | 867 | 721 |
| Finance costs | 131 | 103 |
| Profit before taxation | 736 | 618 |
| Taxation | 88 | 75 |
| Profit for the year | 648 | 543 |

**Weber Limited: Statement of Financial Position**

|  | 20X4 | 20X3 |
|---|---|---|
|  | *£000* | *£000* |
| **ASSETS** | | |
| **Non-current assets** | | |
| Property, plant and equipment | 4,231 | 3,873 |
|  | | |
| **Current assets** | | |
| Inventories | 151 | 137 |
| Trade and other receivables | 606 | 585 |
| Cash | 101 | 86 |
|  | 858 | 808 |
| **Total assets** | 5,089 | 4,681 |
|  | | |
| **EQUITY AND LIABILITIES** | | |
| **Equity** | | |
| Share capital | 2,500 | 2,500 |
| Retained earnings | 491 | 400 |
| **Total equity** | 2,991 | 2,900 |
|  | | |
| **Non-current liabilities** | | |
| Borrowing | 1,850 | 1,550 |
|  | | |
| **Current liabilities** | | |
| Trade and other payables | 248 | 231 |
| **Total liabilities** | 2,098 | 1,781 |
| **Total equity and liabilities** | 5,089 | 4,681 |

**(a)**    Complete the table below by calculating the key indicators (to 2 decimal places) for 20X4 and 20X3 for Weber Limited.

| Weber Limited | 20X4 Indicator | 20X3 Indicator |
|---|---|---|
| Gross profit margin % | | |
| Profit from operations margin % | | |
| Trade payables payment period in days | | |
| Inventory holding period in days | | |
| Current ratio | | |
| Quick ratio | | |

**(b)** You have been asked to prepare points to include in an email to the Chief Credit Controller to assist in his decision whether to give credit to Weber Ltd.

Refer to Weber Ltd's financial statements and the key performance indicators calculated in (a) and complete the points set out below by inserting the appropriate figure or selecting the correct option.

(1) Sales revenue for 20X4 compared to 20X3 has increased by [          ] %

which means that the company may have

**sold fewer units / decreased the unit selling price / experienced an increased demand for its products.**

(2) The gross profit margin has remained constant, which indicates that the company has

**increased the selling price / increased the purchase price / made no change to the selling and purchase price of its product**.

(3) The company is making a **profit / loss** at operational level and the profit from operations margin has **increased / decreased**.

(4) The trade payables payment period measures on average the number of days that **inventory is held / customers take to pay / the company takes to pay its suppliers**. For Weber Ltd this has **risen / fallen** slightly.

(5) The current ratio is **less than 1 / greater than 1**, which is a **sign of insolvency / sign of poor liquidity / good sign**.

(6) The quick ratio is **less than 1 / more than 1** which **is / is not** a major concern in terms of liquidity.

(7) The inventory holding period has remained constant. This is a **good sign / bad sign** and indicates **stability / that inventory could run out / that inventory levels are too low**.

(8) Overall it appears that the company is **solvent / insolvent** and has **sufficient / insufficient** liquidity to pays its liabilities as they fall due.

(9) On the basis of the financial statements that have been provided to us and the key performance indicators, I recommend that **credit be given / credit not be given** to Weber Ltd.

**Task 5**

Lily Limited has been trading with Pascale Direct Limited for several years and has, until recently, always settled Invoices on time. Following several late payments Lily Limited has contacted Pascale Direct Limited to request an increase in their credit limit from £80,000 to £150,000. Lily Limited has supplied the Statement of Profit or Loss below and the Statement of Financial Position on the next page.

**Lily Limited: Statement of Profit or Loss**

|  | 20X3 | 20X2 |
|---|---|---|
|  | £000 | £000 |
| Sales revenue | 10,600 | 5,900 |
| Cost of sales | 7,791 | 3,894 |
| Gross profit | 2,809 | 2,006 |
| Distribution costs | 120 | 67 |
| Administration expenses | 1,414 | 802 |
| Profit from operations | 1,275 | 1,137 |
| Finance costs | 187 | 18 |
| Profit before taxation | 1,088 | 1,119 |
| Taxation | 215 | 249 |
| Profit for the year | 873 | 870 |

**Lily Limited: Statement of Financial Position**

|  | 20X3 | 20X2 |
|---|---|---|
|  | *£000* | *£000* |
| **ASSETS** |  |  |
| **Non-current assets** |  |  |
| Property, plant and equipment | 1,049 | 1,105 |
|  |  |  |
| **Current assets** |  |  |
| Inventories | 652 | 650 |
| Trade and other receivables | 2,846 | 947 |
| Cash | - | 784 |
|  | 3,498 | 2,381 |
| **Total assets** | 4,547 | 3,486 |
|  |  |  |
| **EQUITY AND LIABILITIES** |  |  |
| **Equity** |  |  |
| Share capital | 1,300 | 1,300 |
| Retained earnings | 277 | 938 |
| **Total equity** | 1,577 | 2,238 |
|  |  |  |
| **Non-current liabilities** |  |  |
| Borrowing | 500 | 800 |
|  |  |  |
| **Current liabilities** |  |  |
| Bank overdraft | 698 | - |
| Trade and other payables | 1,772 | 448 |
| **Total liabilities** | 2,970 | 1,248 |
| **Total equity and liabilities** | 4,547 | 3,486 |

The Finance Manager at Pascale Direct Limited has calculated financial indicators from the financial statements provided by Lily Limited.

These indicators are shown at the top of the next page.

| Lily Limited | 20X3 | 20X2 |
| --- | --- | --- |
| Gross profit margin % | 26.5 | 34 |
| Profit from operations margin % | 12.03 | 19.27 |
| Interest cover | 6.82 | 63.17 |
| Current ratio | 1.42 | 5.31 |
| Trade payables payment period in days | 83.02 | 41.99 |
| Trade receivables collection period in days | 98 | 58.59 |
| Inventory holding period in days | 30.55 | 60.93 |
| Gearing % | 43.17 | 26.33 |

A trainee Sales Line Manager of Pascale Direct Limited has reviewed the financial statements provided by Lily Limited and the financial indicators shown above and has made comments suggesting that Lily Limited should be granted an increase in its credit limit. These comments are set out below.

1.  The company turnover has increased by 44.34% from £5.9 million to £10.6 million. This is an excellent sign which shows that the company is expanding.

2.  The gross profit has increased from £2,006,000 to £2,809,000. This means that more cash is available to pay debts.

3.  The profit from operations has increased by £138,000 and the profit after tax has remained the same which is a good sign.

4.  The interest cover is now much better than the previous year, when it was too high.

5.  The current ratio has fallen, but it is still over 1 which means the company is solvent.

6.  The trade receivables have increased by £1,899,000 which is a good sign as it is far less than the increase in turnover of £4,700,000.

7.  The trade payables payment period has increased from 42 days to 83 days; this implies that the company is taking advantage of good credit terms from suppliers.

8.  The inventory has remained the same which is an excellent sign.

9.  Gearing has increased which means that the banks are happy to lend money to this business.

(a)    **You are to** write bullet point notes dealing with the accuracy and validity of each comment that the trainee Sales Line Manager has made.

Use the data available to you in the financial statements and table of financial indicators to support your comments.

**(b)**    **You are to** state whether or not you would recommend granting the increase in credit limit to Lily Limited:

| ✔ | |
|---|---|
| Yes | |
| No | |

**Task 6**

You have been provided with the credit control policy for Barlow Limited. Today's date is 30 April 20X3.

The credit control management procedures are as follows:

1. An order for goods is received by email, fax or phone (all phone calls are recorded).

2. Goods are delivered and a goods received note is signed by the customer.

3. The goods received notes are kept in a file in the accounts office.

4. An invoice will be issued on the day after delivery on 30 day terms.

5. An aged analysis of trade receivables is produced weekly.

6. A reminder telephone is made when the debt is 7 days overdue.

7. When a debt is 14 days overdue a letter is sent.

8. When a debt is 28 days overdue the account will be put on stop.

9. The debt will either be placed in the hands of a debt collection company or legal proceedings could be instigated if the customer does not respond to calls or letters.

10. The business is credit insured, however insurance is only given for customers once they have a history of trade with the business of at least 12 months and have successfully paid for at least three invoiced amounts. Only 80% of the value of the debt is insured. VAT will be reclaimed from HMRC.

   The assistant responsible for credit control has been on secondment to an associate company for several months but you have access to the notes she prepared.

Identify the most appropriate course of action for each customer based on the information provided.

**(a) Tilsley Ltd**

Tilsley Ltd has a history of paying late but they have always paid eventually. There is a balance on the account of £20,700 which relates to one invoice dated 1 March 20X3.

The action needed is:

|  | ✔ |
|---|---|
| (a) The account should be put on stop | |
| (b) The account is not overdue so no action is required | |
| (c) Tilsley Ltd should be contacted and an immediate payment requested | |
| (d) A statement should be sent on 7 May 20X3 | |

**(b)** **Cole Ltd**

This new customer placed its first order a few weeks ago. The goods were delivered on 1 April 20X3 and the invoice was raised on 12 April 20X3 on 30 day terms.

The action needed is:

| | | ✔ |
|---|---|---|
| (a) | The account should be put on stop | |
| (b) | The account is not overdue so no action is required | |
| (c) | Cole Ltd should be contacted and an immediate payment requested | |
| (d) | A statement should have been sent on 19 April 20X3 | |

**(c)** **McDonald Ltd**

McDonald Ltd has gone into administration. The account is not credit insured.

The action needed is to:

| | | ✔ |
|---|---|---|
| (a) | Place the account on stop and contact a debt collection company to deal with processing a claim against McDonald Ltd | |
| (b) | Contact the insolvency service and register a claim with the credit insurer | |
| (c) | Contact the insolvency practitioner and register a claim with the credit insurer | |
| (d) | Contact the insolvency practitioner and make a provision in the accounts | |

**(d)** **Lloyd Ltd**

Lloyd Ltd sent a payment of £7,476 but did not provide details of which invoices relate to the payment.

The action needed is:

| | | ✔ |
|---|---|---|
| (a) | Lloyd Ltd should be contacted to confirm which invoices are being paid so that the unallocated receipt can be allocated | |
| (b) | The £7,476 should be returned to Lloyd Ltd | |
| (c) | The £7,476 should be allocated to the last invoice first | |
| (d) | The account should be put on stop until the payment is allocated | |

**(e)** **Grimshaw Ltd**

Grimshaw Ltd owes a balance of £18,000 including VAT. The account is on stop. Attempts to contact the customer by telephone have been unsuccessful. The account is not credit insured.

Complete the sentence below:

Contact the credit insurer to make a claim for £ [          ], make a provision for

£ [          ] and claim VAT of £ [          ] from HMRC.

**(f)** **Duckworth Ltd**

Duckworth Ltd is a long-established customer with a history of late payments, but it always pays eventually. Duckworth Ltd has an overdue balance of £17,000 due to Barlow Ltd.

The Managing Director of Duckworth Ltd is a personal friend of Barlow Ltd's Managing Director.

The action needed is to:

| | | ✔ |
|---|---|---|
| (a) | Place the account on stop and contact a debt collection company to deal with processing a claim against Duckworth Ltd | |
| (b) | Ask the Managing Director of Barlow Ltd what action should be taken | |
| (c) | Visit the premises of Duckworth Ltd and seize goods to the value of the outstanding balance | |
| (d) | Put a claim in to the credit insurance company for the overdue amounts | |

**Task 7**

Stable Ltd supplies goods to the manufacturing sector. You work in the Credit Control Department and the date is 31 July 20X3, the company's financial year-end.

The Senior Credit Controller is away on holiday but has left you a copy of the company's credit control policy together with notes on some of the customer accounts.

An extract of these notes is provided below.

---

**Stable Ltd - Notes on credit control procedure**

1. An order for goods is received by email, fax or phone (all phone calls are recorded).

2. Goods are delivered and a goods received note is signed by the customer.

3. The goods received notes are kept in a file in the accounts office.

4. An invoice will be issued on the day after delivery on 30 day terms.

5. An aged analysis of trade receivables is produced weekly.

6. A reminder telephone call is made when the debt is 7 days overdue.

7. When a debt is 14 days overdue a letter is sent.

8. When a debt is 28 days overdue the account will be put on stop.

9. The debt will either be placed in the hands of a debt collection company or legal proceedings could be instigated if the customer does not respond to calls or letters.

10. The business is credit insured, however insurance is only given for customers once they have a history of trade with the business of at least 12 months and have successfully paid for at least three invoiced amounts. Only 70% of the value of the debt is insured.

11. All sales invoices Include VAT at the standard rate of 20% and VAT is recovered from HMRC under its Bad Debt Relief Scheme where applicable.

---

**(a)**   **You are to** review the information provided for each of three customers of Stable Ltd on the next two pages and prepare a list of actions for collecting the outstanding amounts due to Stable Ltd.

Your list of actions should include a summary of the options available for the company to pursue and recommendations for provisions or write-off of irrecoverable debts where appropriate.

**Magnum Ltd**

The sales ledger of Magnum Ltd shows a balance outstanding of £15,600 which is now 90 days overdue. All letters and telephone calls have been ignored.

**Hudsons Inc**

Hudsons Inc is an overseas customer with a credit limit of £50,000; they have just placed an order for £35,000 and have an existing balance on the sales ledger of £25,000.

**Shoreline Ltd**

Shoreline Ltd has a balance outstanding of £33,240, which is made up of an invoice for £29,400 dated 30 June 20X3 and an invoice for £3,840 dated 31 May 20X3. Shoreline Ltd is a regular customer and usually pays on time.

**(b)    Sheila Mary Ltd**

The sales ledger account for Sheila Mary Ltd has become corrupted but the following information is available:

- Balance 1 June 20X3 - £165,000
- Invoices raised: 8 June 20X3 £60,000 plus VAT at 20%, 15 July 20X3 £67,200 (VAT inclusive)
- Credit notes raised: 6 June 20X3 £3,000 (VAT inclusive), 17 July 20X3 £5,520 (VAT inclusive)
- Bank receipts: 5 June 20X3 £162,000, 20 July 20X3 £72,000

**You are to** calculate the balances on the account of Sheila Mary Ltd at 30 June 20X3 and 31 July 20X3.

**(c)** **Sweet Pea Ltd**

No action has been taken in respect of the account for Sweet Pea Ltd, who have an agreed credit limit of £20,000. The account transactions are listed below, and today's date is 31 July 20X3:

- Invoice of £5,000 plus VAT at 20% on 1 May 20X3
- Invoice of £16,000 plus VAT at 20% on 1 June 20X3

Identify the actions, with dates, that should have been undertaken by the credit control team at Stable Ltd:

# Practice assessment 3

**Task 1**

**(a)** An acceptance of an offer must be:

| | | ✔ |
|---|---|---|
| (a) | Unconditional | |
| (b) | Conditional | |
| (c) | Made at the same time as the consideration | |

Tick the **one** correct option.

**(b)** An offer in contract for the sale of goods may be terminated when:

| | | ✔ |
|---|---|---|
| (a) | A counter offer is made | |
| (b) | The goods are found to be faulty | |
| (c) | The price is unacceptable | |

Tick the **one** correct option.

**(c)** The Data Protection Act gives protection for information relating to:

| | | ✔ |
|---|---|---|
| (a) | Only individuals | |
| (b) | Only limited companies | |
| (c) | Both individuals and limited companies | |

Tick the **one** correct option.

**(d)**   Mario offers to buy a signed photograph of the famous actress Scarlett Johansson from a friend. He does not have much money so the friend as a favour lets him have it for £5 when in fact it could sell for over £100. The situation in contract law is that:

| | | ✔ |
|---|---|---|
| (a) | The £5 is sufficient consideration even if a very low price is set as a favour to the buyer | |
| (b) | The £5 is not sufficient consideration because the price does not reflect the true value of the photograph | |
| (c) | Mario now owes his friend £95 | |

Tick the **one** correct option.

**(e)**   Otto tells his daughter Cordelia that he is leaving her £5,000 in his will. The next day Otto falls off a ladder and is tragically killed. Cordelia then spends £3,000 on computer equipment for the business she runs, relying on the fact that the £5,000 will be coming to her. It turns out that the amount left in the will to Cordelia was actually only £500. Cordelia wants to know what her legal position is and if there is a contract. The correct advice would be:

| | | ✔ |
|---|---|---|
| (a) | There is no valid contract because the agreement was a domestic one and not intended to create legal relations | |
| (b) | There is no valid contract because Otto has died | |
| (c) | There is a valid contract and Cordelia is entitled to put in a claim to the solicitors dealing with Otto's will | |

Tick the **one** correct option.

**(f)**   The following situation is an example of a person who sues for damages:

| | | ✔ |
|---|---|---|
| (a) | A person who takes legal action in the courts for completion of a contract for laying a patio | |
| (b) | A person who takes legal action in the courts for money compensation for breach of contract | |
| (c) | A person who seeks compensation in the courts for damaged goods | |

Tick the **one** correct option.

**(g)**   The Late Payments of Commercial Debts (Interest) Act allows small companies to charge interest to customers who exceed their credit terms and pay late. The interest charge is based on the current bank base rate.

**You are to** enter in the box below the percentage rate charged.

If the current base rate is 1.25%, the late payment interest rate is ⬚ per cent.

**(h)**   A customer owes £7,000 (excluding VAT @ 20%) and the debt is 60 days late.

**You are to** calculate the interest charge under the Late Payments of Commercial Debts (Interest) Act to the nearest penny. Enter the figure in the box below. The bank base rate is 1.5%.

£ ⬚

**(i)**   **You are to** enter each of the following words or phrases into the correct box within the text which follows.

**satisfactory quality**     **intend**     **fit for the purpose**     **delivery**     **described**

The Sale of Goods Act states that any purchaser should expect goods purchased to be of

⬚ ,   as   ⬚   and

⬚ .   Title to the goods passes to the purchaser when the

parties to the contract ⬚ that it should, normally this will be on

⬚ .

**Task 2**

**(a)**    Your business is assessing the credit status of a new customer who has applied for 30 day credit and a limit of £20,000. You have sent off for a banker's reference. The answer comes back "Should prove good for your figures and purpose." This means:

✔

| | | |
|---|---|---|
| (a) | The bank is not fully sure and hints that further enquiries should be made | |
| (b) | The customer is undoubted and a good credit risk | |
| (c) | No credit should be given | |

Tick the **one** correct option.

**(b)**    A business wanting to encourage a good customer who is also a bad payer to pay up is most likely to:

✔

| | | |
|---|---|---|
| (a) | Put the account on stop | |
| (b) | Reduce the customer's credit limit | |
| (c) | Contact the customer by telephone and discuss the matter | |

Tick **one** option.

**(c)**    A business has a £20,000 debt outstanding on a customer account. The situation is very simple and the case will be concluded within one day. Which County Court process would deal with this size of debt?

✔

| | | |
|---|---|---|
| (a) | Small Claims Track | |
| (b) | Fast Track | |
| (c) | Multi Track | |

Tick the **one** correct option.

**(d)** A warrant of delivery is:

✔

| | | |
|---|---|---|
| (a) | An order for the court bailiffs to enter the property of the customer who owes money to the seller to seize valuable assets | |
| (b) | An order which will authorise an employer to deduct regular amounts from the customer's salary in order to repay the debt | |
| (c) | An order for the court bailiffs to seize goods belonging to the seller and held by a customer who owes money to the seller | |

Tick the **one** correct option.

**(e)** A statutory demand is:

✔

| | | |
|---|---|---|
| (a) | A court order for the repayment of a debt | |
| (b) | A request by the court to attend a bankruptcy hearing | |
| (c) | A formal demand for at least £750 made by the person or company owed money | |

Tick the **one** correct option.

**(f)** A bankruptcy order can be issued by the court against:

✔

| | | |
|---|---|---|
| (a) | An individual | |
| (b) | A private limited company | |
| (c) | A public limited company | |

Tick the **one** correct option.

**(g)** You are a trade supplier owed money by Dufco Ltd, which has recently been put into administration. This company owes a great deal of money to the bank. In this case you should:

|  |  | ✔ |
|---|---|---|
| (a) | Get paid after the bank gets its money back | |
| (b) | Make a statutory claim to get your money back | |
| (c) | Try to recover the money and hope that the company recovers | |

Tick the **one** appropriate option.

**(h)** Aldridge Ltd's standard credit terms of payment are 30 days. It offers to customers an early settlement discount of 2.5% for payment within 7 days of invoice.

The simple annual interest rate of the discount is: ⬚ per cent.

Calculations should be to two decimal places.

**(i)** Brunning Ltd is a regular customer of Butcher Ltd. During the year Brunning Ltd bought from Butcher Ltd 23,010 items which cost £44 each, including VAT at 20%. At the end of the year Brunning Ltd's balance of account was £112,500.

The receivables collection period (to the nearest day) is: ⬚ days.

**Task 3**

You work as a Credit Control Manager for Purple Planet Ltd which uses a credit rating system to assess the credit status of new customers. The credit rating (scoring) system is used to assess the risk of default by calculating key indicators (ratios), comparing them to the table and calculating an aggregate score. This system is set out below.

| Credit rating (scoring ) system | Score |
|---|---|
| **Profit from operations margin** | |
| Losses | −5 |
| Less than 5% | 0 |
| 5% and above but less than 10% | 5 |
| 10% and above but less than 20% | 10 |
| 20% or more | 20 |
| **Interest cover** | |
| No cover | −30 |
| Less than 1 | −20 |
| 1 and above but less than 2 | −10 |
| 2 and above but less than 4 | 0 |
| 4 or more | 10 |
| **Liquidity ratio** | |
| Less than 1 | −20 |
| 1 and above but less than 1.25 | −10 |
| 1.25 and above but less than 1.5 | 0 |
| 1.5 or more | 10 |
| **Gearing (total debt / total debt plus equity)** | |
| Less than 25% | 20 |
| 25% and above but less than 50% | 10 |
| 50% and above but less than 65% | 0 |
| 65% and above but less than 75% | −20 |
| 75% and above but less than 80% | −40 |
| 80% or more | −100 |

| Risk | Aggregate score |
|------|-----------------|
| Very low risk | Between 60 and 21 |
| Low risk | Between 20 and 1 |
| Medium risk | Between 0 and –24 |
| High risk | Between –25 and –50 |
| Very high risk | Between –50 and –160 |

The Sales Department has asked for a credit limit of £55,000 to be given to Garden Design Limited, a new customer.

The financial statements that follow have been supplied by Garden Design Limited.

### Garden Design Limited: Statement of Profit or Loss

|  | 20X2 | 20X1 |
|---|---|---|
|  | £000 | £000 |
| Sales revenue | 7,500 | 6,300 |
| Cost of sales | 3,639 | 3,654 |
| Gross profit | 3,861 | 2,646 |
| Distribution costs | 758 | 687 |
| Administration expenses | 1,978 | 2,211 |
| Profit / (loss) from operations | 1,125 | (252) |
| Finance costs | 35 | 45 |
| Profit / (loss) before taxation | 1,090 | (297) |
| Taxation | 220 | - |
| Profit / (loss) for the year | 870 | (297) |

**Garden Design Limited: Statement of Financial Position**

|  | 20X2 | 20X1 |
|---|---|---|
|  | *£000* | *£000* |
| **ASSETS** |  |  |
| **Non-current assets** |  |  |
| Property, plant and equipment | 2,004 | 1,231 |
|  |  |  |
| **Current assets** |  |  |
| Inventories | 151 | 148 |
| Trade and other receivables | 1,221 | 998 |
| Cash | 55 | 486 |
|  | 1,427 | 1,632 |
| **Total assets** | 3,431 | 2,863 |
|  |  |  |
| **EQUITY AND LIABILITIES** |  |  |
| **Equity** |  |  |
| Share capital | 1,500 | 800 |
| Retained earnings | 360 | 35 |
| **Total equity** | 1,860 | 835 |
|  |  |  |
| **Non-current liabilities** |  |  |
| Borrowing | 1,000 | 1,600 |
|  |  |  |
| **Current liabilities** |  |  |
| Trade and other payables | 571 | 428 |
| **Total liabilities** | 1,571 | 2,028 |
| **Total equity and liabilities** | 3,431 | 2,863 |

**(a)**  Complete the table below by calculating the key indicators (to 2 decimal places) for 20X2 and 20X1 for Garden Design Limited, and assess the company using the credit rating scoring system.

| Garden Design Limited | 20X2 Indicator | 20X2 Rating | 20X1 Indicator | 20X1 Rating |
|---|---|---|---|---|
| Profit from operations margin % | | | | |
| Interest cover | | | | |
| Quick ratio | | | | |
| Gearing % | | | | |
| Total credit rating | | | | |

**(b)** Based on the results of your credit rating and using the table below, recommend whether the requested credit limit should be given to Garden Design Limited.

| Rating | Decision |
|---|---|
| Very low or low risk current year and very low or low risk previous year | Accept |
| Very low or low risk current year and medium risk previous year | Accept |
| Very low or low risk current year and high or very high risk previous year | Request latest management accounts and defer decision |
| Very high risk or high risk current year | Reject |
| Medium risk current year and medium, low or very low risk previous year | Accept |
| Medium risk current year and high or very high risk previous year | Request latest management accounts and defer decision |

| Credit decision | ✔ |
|---|---|
| (a) Accept | |
| (b) Reject | |
| (c) Request latest management accounts and defer decision | |

**Task 4**

The Sales Department has asked for a credit limit of £18,000 to be given to Joseph Limited who is a potential new customer.

The financial statements that follow have been supplied by Joseph Limited.

**Joseph Limited: Statement of Profit or Loss**

|  | 20X3 | 20X2 |
|---|---|---|
|  | *£000* | *£000* |
| Sales revenue | 6,124 | 4,536 |
| Cost of sales | 4,284 | 3,183 |
| Gross profit | 1,840 | 1,353 |
| Distribution costs | 306 | 181 |
| Administration expenses | 919 | 723 |
| Profit from operations | 615 | 449 |
| Finance costs | 38 | 10 |
| Profit before taxation | 577 | 439 |
| Taxation | 120 | 90 |
| Profit for the year | 457 | 349 |

**Joseph Limited: Statement of Financial Position**

|  | 20X3 | 20X2 |
|---|---|---|
|  | *£000* | *£000* |
| **ASSETS** |  |  |
| **Non-current assets** |  |  |
| Property, plant and equipment | 2,520 | 1,381 |
|  |  |  |
| **Current assets** |  |  |
| Inventories | 328 | 392 |
| Trade and other receivables | 684 | 435 |
| Cash | - | 27 |
|  | 1,012 | 854 |
| **Total assets** | 3,532 | 2,235 |
|  |  |  |
| **EQUITY AND LIABILITIES** |  |  |
| **Equity** |  |  |
| Share capital | 1,250 | 1,000 |
| Retained earnings | 308 | 496 |
| **Total equity** | 1,558 | 1,496 |
|  |  |  |
| **Non-current liabilities** |  |  |
| Borrowing | 850 | 250 |
|  |  |  |
| **Current liabilities** |  |  |
| Borrowings | 56 | - |
| Trade and other payables | 1,068 | 489 |
| **Total liabilities** | 1,974 | 739 |
| **Total equity and liabilities** | 3,532 | 2,235 |

**(a)** Complete the table below by calculating the key indicators (to 2 decimal places) for 20X3 and 20X2 for Joseph Limited.

| Joseph Limited | 20X3 Indicator | 20X2 Indicator |
|---|---|---|
| Gross profit margin % | | |
| Profit from operations margin % | | |
| Trade payables payment period in days | | |
| Inventory holding period in days | | |
| Current ratio | | |
| Quick ratio | | |

**(b)** You have been asked to prepare points to include in an email to the Chief Credit Controller to assist in his decision whether to give credit to Joseph Limited.

Refer to Joseph Limited's financial statements and the key performance indicators calculated in (a) and complete the points set out below by inserting the appropriate figure or selecting the correct option.

(1) Sales revenue for 20X3 compared to 20X2 has increased by [      ] %

which means that the company may have

**sold fewer units / decreased the unit selling price / either sold more units or increased the selling price of its product**.

(2) Gross profit has increased by [      ] % and profit from operations has

increased by [      ] %.

Both the gross profit margin and the profit from operations margin have **increased / decreased** slightly.

(3) The current ratio provides a rough measure of the **long-term solvency / short-term solvency / insolvency** of the organisation.

In the case of Joseph Limited it has **risen / fallen** and is now **less than 1 / greater than 1**, which is a **sign of insolvency / sign of poor liquidity / good sign**.

(4) The inventory level has **increased / decreased**; this is a **good sign / bad sign** as the inventory holding period has **increased / decreased**, which may mean that **inventory could run out / inventory levels are too high**.

(5) The quick ratio has **fallen / risen** which **is / is not** a major concern and indicates **poor / good** liquidity.

(6) The trade payables payment period has **increased / decreased** by [      ] days. It appears that the company is **able / finding it more difficult** to pay its liabilities as they fall due.

(7) On the basis of the financial statements that have been provided to us and the key performance indicators I recommend that **credit be given / credit not be given** to Joseph Limited.

**Task 5**

Berry Limited has been trading with Hollywood Limited for several years and has usually kept within its limit. Recently, however, the company has needed chasing for payment of its invoices.

The company has now contacted Hollywood Limited to request an increase in its credit limit from £50,000 to £75,000.

Berry Limited has supplied the financial statements that follow but the figures for 20X3 have not yet been sent to Hollywood Limited.

**Berry Limited: Statement of Profit or Loss**

|  | 20X2 | 20X1 |
|---|---|---|
|  | £000 | £000 |
| Sales revenue | 5,170 | 4,575 |
| Cost of sales | 2,068 | 1,830 |
| Gross profit | 3,102 | 2,745 |
| Distribution costs | 620 | 549 |
| Administration expenses | 2,747 | 1,693 |
| Profit / (loss) from operations | (265) | 503 |
| Finance costs | - | 10 |
| Profit / (loss) before taxation | (265) | 493 |
| Taxation | - | 81 |
| Profit / (loss) for the year | (265) | 412 |

**Berry Limited: Statement of Financial Position**

|  | 20X2 | 20X1 |
|---|---|---|
|  | £000 | £000 |
| **ASSETS** | | |
| **Non-current assets** | | |
| Property, plant and equipment | 2,984 | 1,056 |
| | | |
| **Current assets** | | |
| Inventories | 283 | 266 |
| Trade and other receivables | 708 | 626 |
| Cash | 252 | 186 |
| | 1,243 | 1,078 |
| **Total assets** | 4,227 | 2,134 |
| | | |
| **EQUITY AND LIABILITIES** | | |
| **Equity** | | |
| Share capital | 3,800 | 1,200 |
| Retained earnings | 195 | 488 |
| **Total equity** | 3,995 | 1,688 |
| | | |
| **Non-current liabilities** | | |
| Borrowing | - | 200 |
| | | |
| Trade and other payables | 232 | 246 |
| **Total liabilities** | 232 | 446 |
| **Total equity and liabilities** | 4,227 | 2,134 |

The credit analysis team at Hollywood Limited has calculated financial indicators from the financial statements provided by Berry Limited.

These indicators are shown at the top of the next page.

| Berry Limited | 20X2 | 20X1 |
|---|---|---|
| Gross profit margin % | 60 | 60 |
| Profit from operations margin % | −5.13 | 10.99 |
| Interest cover | No cover | 50.3 |
| Current ratio | 5.36 | 4.38 |
| Trade payables payment period in days | 40.95 | 49.07 |
| Trade receivables collection period in days | 49.98 | 49.94 |
| Inventory holding period in days | 49.95 | 53.05 |
| Gearing % | N/A | 10.59 |

The Sales Manager of Hollywood Limited has reviewed the information provided by Berry Limited and has made the comments listed below. He is not keen on the proposition and reluctant to give the increase requested by Berry Limited.

1. The company turnover has increased by 13.01% from £4,575,000 to £5,170,000. This is a good sign.

2. The profit from operations has decreased by £768,000. This means that less cash is available to pay debts.

3. There is no interest cover which means that the company is in a worse position than last year.

4. The current ratio should be 2 which means in both years it is too high.

5. The trade receivables have increased by £82,000 which means the company is overtrading.

6. The trade payables payment period is down from 49.07 days to 40.95 days which implies that the company is struggling to obtain credit from its suppliers.

7. Inventory has increased which supports the conclusion of overtrading.

8. Gearing has decreased which means that the banks are not happy to lend money to the business.

(a) **You are to** write brief bullet point notes dealing with the accuracy and validity of each comment that the Sales Manager has made.

Use the data available to you in the financial statements and table of financial indicators to support your comments.

**(b)**    Indicate below which course of action you would recommend.    ✔

| (a) | Increased credit should be given | |
|-----|----------------------------------|---|
| (b) | Increased credit should not be given | |
| (c) | Request up-to-date management accounts and details of the equity injection made in 20X2 before granting credit | |

**Task 6**

You have been provided with the credit control policy for Austen Limited. Today's date is 31 October 20X3.

Current credit control procedures for dealing with customer accounts are as follows:

1.      An order for goods is received by email, fax or phone (all phone calls are recorded).

2.      Goods are delivered and a goods received note is signed by the customer.

3.      The goods received notes are kept in a file in the accounts office.

4.      An invoice will be issued on the day after delivery on 30 day terms.

5.      An aged analysis of trade receivables is produced weekly.

6.      A statement is sent when the account is 7 days overdue.

7.      When a debt is 14 days overdue a reminder telephone call is made.

8.      When a debt is 21 days overdue a final reminder letter is sent.

9.      When a debt is 28 days overdue the account will be put on stop.

10.     The debt will either be placed in the hands of a debt collection company or legal proceedings could be instigated if the customer does not respond to calls or letters.

11.     The business is credit insured, however insurance is only given for customers once they have a history of trade with the business of at least 12 months and have successfully paid for at least three invoiced amounts. Only 80% of the value of the debt is insured. VAT will be reclaimed from HMRC.

You are new to the job but you have ready access to the above list of procedures to be followed when chasing up customer accounts.

You have also printed out the aged receivables analysis as at 31 October 20X3:

| Customer | Balance £ | 0-30 days £ | 31-60 days £ | 61-90 days £ | Over 90 days £ |
|---|---|---|---|---|---|
| Clarke Ltd | 72,000 | | 72,000 | | |
| Day Ltd | 17,400 | | | 17,400 | |
| Horwood Ltd | 180,000 | 60,000 | 60,000 | 60,000 | |
| Rhodes Ltd | 678 | | | | 678 |
| Stein Ltd | 115,200 | 115,200 | | | |

**You are to** identify the most appropriate course of action for each of the following customers, based on the information provided.

**(a)    Clarke Ltd**

The balance on Clarke Ltd's account consists of one invoice dated 14 September 20X3.

The action needed is:

✔

| | | |
|---|---|---|
| (a) | The account should be put on stop | |
| (b) | The account is not overdue so no action is required | |
| (c) | A final reminder letter should be sent on 4 November 20X3 | |
| (d) | A statement should be sent on 31 October 20X3 | |

**(b)    Day Ltd**

Day Ltd is a long established customer who always pays on time. A payment received of £17,400 has been posted to the unallocated payments account in the purchase ledger.

The action needed is:

✔

| | | |
|---|---|---|
| (a) | The account should be put on stop | |
| (b) | Establish that the payment was from Day Ltd, credit Day Ltd with £17,400 and debit unallocated payments with £17,400 | |
| (c) | Credit Day Ltd with £17,400 and debit unallocated payments with £17,400 | |
| (d) | Establish that the payment was from Day Ltd, debit Day Ltd with £17,400 and credit unallocated payments with £17,400 | |

**(c)    Horwood Ltd**

Horwood Ltd has gone into administration. The account is credit insured.

The action needed is to:

✔

| | | |
|---|---|---|
| (a) | Place the account on stop and contact a debt collection company to deal with processing a claim against Horwood Ltd | |
| (b) | Contact the insolvency service and register a claim with the credit insurer | |
| (c) | Contact the insolvency practitioner and register a claim with the credit insurer | |
| (d) | Contact the insolvency practitioner and make a provision in the accounts | |

**(d)** **Rhodes Ltd**

Rhodes Ltd is no longer a customer, the account is on stop. Attempts to contact Rhodes Ltd by telephone and letter have been unsuccessful. The amount is not credit insured.

The action needed is:

| | | ✔ |
|---|---|---|
| (a) | Visit the premises of Rhodes Ltd and seize goods to the value of the outstanding balance | |
| (b) | Put a claim in to the credit insurance company for the overdue amounts | |
| (c) | Refer the debt to a debt collection agency and make a provision in the accounts | |
| (d) | Make a provision in the accounts | |

**(e)** **Stein Ltd**

This is a new customer who placed its first order a few weeks ago. The goods were delivered on 1 October 20X3 and the invoice raised on 4 October 20X3 on 30 day terms.

The action needed is:

| | | ✔ |
|---|---|---|
| (a) | The account should be put on stop | |
| (b) | The account is not overdue so no action is required | |
| (c) | Stein Ltd should be contacted and an immediate payment requested | |
| (d) | A phone call should have been made on 18 October 20X3 and a letter sent on 25 October 20X3 | |

**Task 7**

Opto Ltd supplies goods to the manufacturing sector. Each product is stamped with a batch number so that they can be easily identified. The standard terms and conditions printed on the back of every sales invoice raised by Moss Ltd include a retention of title clause. There is also a clause that states that problems with goods must be notified to Moss Ltd within 24 hours of delivery. Goods returned are subject to a restocking fee of 10%.

You work in the Credit Control Department and the date is 30 June 20X3, the company's financial year-end.

The Senior Credit Controller is away on holiday in Italy but has left you a copy of the company's credit control policy together with notes on how to deal with the customer accounts. The notes are as follows:

---

**Credit control summary notes**

1.  An order for goods is received by email, fax or phone (all phone calls are recorded).

2.  Goods are delivered and a goods received note is signed by the customer.

3.  The goods received notes are kept in a file in the accounts office.

4.  An invoice will be issued on the day after delivery on 30 day terms.

5.  An aged analysis of trade receivables is produced weekly.

6.  A reminder telephone call is made when the debt is 7 days overdue.

7.  When a debt is 14 days overdue a letter is sent.

8.  When a debt is 28 days overdue the account will be put on stop.

9.  The debt will either be placed in the hands of a debt collection company or legal proceedings could be instigated if the customer does not respond to calls or letters.

10. The business is credit insured, however insurance is only given for customers once they have a history of trade with the business of at least 12 months and have successfully paid for at least three invoiced amounts. Only 70% of the value of the debt is insured.

11. All sales invoices include VAT at the standard rate of 20% and VAT is recovered from HMRC under its Bad Debt Relief Scheme where applicable.

---

**You are to:**

**(a)**   Review the information provided for each of the three customers below and prepare an action plan for each customer for collecting the outstanding amounts due to Opto Ltd.

Your action plan should include a summary of the options available for the company to pursue and recommendations for provisions or write-off of irrecoverable debts where appropriate.

**Beck Ltd**

Beck Ltd has an amount owing of £3,000 and the debt is over 90 days old. There is no dispute with the order; Beck Ltd is simply refusing to pay.

**Free Ltd**

Free Ltd has gone into receivership owing Opto Ltd £15,000 (including VAT). Free Ltd has contacted the receiver who has stated that it is unlikely that the retention of title will be valid because the company purchased similar items from several suppliers and therefore the goods are not identified as being supplied by Opto Ltd.

The receiver also stated that the existing debt will be classed as an unsecured creditor by Free Ltd.

**Hardy Ltd**

Hardy Ltd is a new customer and no credit limit has been allowed. Hardy Ltd paid for goods by cheque when the order was made. The order was processed before the cheque had cleared and the cheque has subsequently bounced. The phone line to Hardy Ltd now appears to have been disconnected.

**(b)    Monte Ltd**

The sales ledger account held for Monte Ltd is not up-to-date because of a flood in the accounts office. The following information has been gathered together:

Balance of Monte Ltd Account on 1 May 20X3:  £105,000

Invoices raised: 8 May 20X3 £40,000 plus VAT at 20%, 16 June 20X3 £78,000 (VAT inclusive)

Credit notes raised: 10 May 20X3 £18,000 (VAT inclusive) subject to a restocking fee of 10%, 26 June 20X3 £4,800 (VAT inclusive) not subject to a restocking fee

Bank receipts: 10 May 20X3 £100,000, 10 June 20X3 £30,000

What is the balance on the account of Monte Ltd at 31 May 20X3 and 30 June 20X3?

**(c)** **Oliver Ltd**

No action has been taken in respect of the account for Oliver Ltd, who have an agreed credit limit of £10,000. The account transactions are listed below, and today's date is 30 June 20X3:

Invoice of £3,000 plus VAT at 20% on 1 March 20X3

Invoice of £2,500 plus VAT at 20% on 2 May 20X3

Identify the actions, with dates, that should have been undertaken by the credit control team at Opto Ltd:

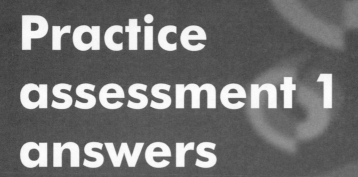

# Practice
# assessment 1
# answers

**Task 1**

**(a)** (c) By the buyer or by the seller

**(b)** (c) Offer, acceptance, consideration, an intention to create legal relations

**(c)** (a) Of satisfactory quality

(c) Fit for the purpose

**(d)** (c) An invitation to treat

**(e)** (c) An offer

**(f)** (c) The terms of the contract are not fulfilled

**(g)** 8.5 per cent

**(h)** £73.97

**(i)** The Data Protection Act protects data held about **individuals** and not **companies**. It covers both computer-based and **manual** records. It is based around eight guiding **principles** which protect the data held.

**Task 2**

**(a)** (b) A credit rating agency

**(b)** (b) A clearly set out and comprehensive credit control policy

**(c)** (c) Small Claims Track

**(d)** (a) A court order sent to a third party such as a bank which has an account for the customer requiring the money to be paid direct to the seller

**(e)** (b) A limited company

**(f)** (a) £750

**(g)** (a) The situation where a company having solvency problems is placed in the hands of an Administrator appointed by the court; the administration process helps to protect the business and will try to return it to solvency

**(h)** 37.06 per cent

**(i)** 30 days

**Task 3**

**(a)**

| Sunny Limited | 20X3 Indicator | 20X3 Rating | 20X2 Indicator | 20X2 Rating |
|---|---|---|---|---|
| Profit from operations margin % | 15 | 10 | 20 | 20 |
| Interest cover | 17.5 | 10 | 10 | 10 |
| Quick ratio | 1.6 | 10 | 1.4 | 0 |
| Gearing % | 41.62 | 10 | 51.75 | 0 |
| Total credit rating | | 40 | | 30 |

**Workings**:

| | Formula | 20X3 | 20X2 |
|---|---|---|---|
| Profit from operations margin % | $\dfrac{\text{Profit from operations x 100}}{\text{Sales revenue}}$ | $\dfrac{630 \times 100}{4,200} = 15\%$ | $\dfrac{770 \times 100}{3,850} = 20\%$ |
| Interest cover | $\dfrac{\text{Profit from operations}}{\text{Interest payable}}$ | $\dfrac{630}{36} = 17.5$ | $\dfrac{770}{77} = 10$ |
| Quick ratio | $\dfrac{\text{Current assets less inventories}}{\text{Current liabilities}}$ | $\dfrac{1,868 - 68}{380 + 745} = 1.6$ | $\dfrac{2,154 - 54}{505 + 995} = 1.4$ |
| Gearing % | $\dfrac{\text{Total debt x 100}}{\text{Total debt plus equity}}$ | $\dfrac{1,230^* \times 100}{1,230 + 1,725} = 41.62\%$   *850 + 380 | $\dfrac{1,555^{**} \times 100}{1,555 + 1,450} = 51.75\%$   **1,050+505 |

**(b)** (a) Accept

**Task 4**

    **(a)**

| Howard Limited | 20X2 Indicator | 20X1 Indicator |
|---|---|---|
| Gross profit margin % | 38.11 | 40.86 |
| Profit from operations margin % | −9.43 | 2.43 |
| Trade payables payment period in days | 72.12 | 49.96 |
| Inventory holding period in days | 39.1 | 32.91 |
| Current ratio | 1.16 | 2.3 |
| Quick ratio | 0.66 | 1.64 |

**Workings**:

| | Formula | 20X2 | 20X1 |
|---|---|---|---|
| Gross profit margin % | $\dfrac{\text{Gross profit} \times 100}{\text{Sales revenue}}$ | $\dfrac{667 \times 100}{1{,}750} = 38.11\%$ | $\dfrac{858 \times 100}{2{,}100} = 40.86\%$ |
| Profit from operations margin % | $\dfrac{\text{Profit from operations} \times 100}{\text{Sales revenue}}$ | $\dfrac{(165) \times 100}{1{,}750} = -9.43\%$ | $\dfrac{51 \times 100}{2{,}100} = 2.43\%$ |
| Trade payables pmt period in days | $\dfrac{\text{Trade payables} \times 365}{\text{Cost of sales}}$ | $\dfrac{214 \times 365}{1{,}083} = 72.12$ | $\dfrac{170 \times 365}{1{,}242} = 49.96$ |
| Inventory holding period in days | $\dfrac{\text{Inventories} \times 365}{\text{Cost of sales}}$ | $\dfrac{116 \times 365}{1{,}083} = 39.1$ | $\dfrac{112 \times 365}{1{,}242} = 32.91$ |
| Current ratio | $\dfrac{\text{Current assets}}{\text{Current liabilities}}$ | $\dfrac{268}{17 + 214} = 1.16$ | $\dfrac{391}{170} = 2.3$ |
| Quick ratio | $\dfrac{\text{Current assets less inventories}}{\text{Current liabilities}}$ | $\dfrac{268 - 116}{17 + 214} = 0.66$ | $\dfrac{391 - 112}{170} = 1.64$ |

**(b)**    (1)    Sales revenue for 20X2 compared to 20X1 has decreased by **16.67%**, which means that the company may have **sold fewer units.**

(2)    The gross profit margin has **decreased** which means that the company has **increased the purchase price.**

(3)    At operational level the company is making a **loss** which **may be a problem depending on the cash flow of the business.**

(4)    The current ratio measures **short-term solvency** of an organisation. In this case it has **decreased** and is **still greater than 1**, which is **a good sign.**

(5)    The quick ratio has **fallen** to 0.66 which **is** a major concern in terms of liquidity.

(6)    The inventory holding period has **increased**. This may mean that inventory **is slow moving.**

(7)    The trade payables payment period has **increased** by **22.16** days. This may indicate that the company has **insufficient** liquidity and is **unlikely** to pays its liabilities as they fall due.

(8)    On the basis of the financial statements that have been provided to us and the key performance indicators I recommend that **credit not be given** to Howard Ltd.

**Workings:**

(1)    Decrease in revenue: $(1,750 - 2,100) / 2,100 = -16.67\%$

(7)    Increase in trade payables payment period: $72.12 - 49.96 = 22.16$ days

**Task 5 (a)**

> **The company's turnover has increased by 25.14% from £4,785,000 to £5,988,000. This is a strong sign of overtrading.**
> - You are correct that the turnover has increased by 25.14% (£1,203,000 / £4,785,000).
> - The fact that turnover has increased significantly is not a strong sign of overtrading as many other indicators have to be considered to decide whether the business is overtrading.
> - These include significant increases in turnover linked to reduced margins, increased levels of current assets and trade cycle days and reduction in cash flow.
> - These points will be considered below.
>
> **The profit from operations has increased by £359,000. This means that more cash is available to pay debts.**
> - You are correct that profit from operations has increased, but the increase is £463,000 not £359,000.
> - This does not mean that more cash is available to pay debts; it depends on where the profit has gone in the period.
> - Has it been "invested" or is it "tied up" in inventory, trade receivables or non-current assets?
> - This is why it is necessary to consider the liquidity of the business and changes in the assets and liabilities to confirm the liquidity of the business.
> - The profit from operations margin has increased by 8.17% which may indicate that the business has not chased turnover at the expense of profits.
> - The gross profit margin has remained constant at 45%, which is a positive sign.
> - Even though there has been a significant increase in sales revenue, the administration expenses have remained roughly the same, which has meant that the profit for the year has increased significantly.
>
> **The interest cover has increased which means that the company is in a worse position than last year.**
> - You are correct in the fact that the interest cover has increased, however, this means that the company is in a better position than last year, not a worse position.
> - Interest cover is a key indicator that is often used by credit agencies and financial institutions.
> - The interest cover is a calculation of how many times the profit from operations can cover the interest payments.
> - The calculation of 7.98 times indicates that the finance costs are covered by the profit from operations by almost 8 times.
> - This is an improvement on the previous year, where there was no cover at all.
> - However, care needs to be taken because, as we may see later, profit from operations does not necessarily equate to the change in cash in the period.
> - Cash generation is needed to pay interest. Many profitable companies go into liquidation because they cannot generate cash.
>
> **The current ratio should be 2 which means that last year the company was insolvent, but this year the company is solvent.**
> - Referring to the fact that the current ratio should be 2 is a common misunderstanding; an acceptable current ratio very much depends on the organisation itself and the type of industry to which it belongs.

- When assessing the credit worthiness of a business the higher the current ratio the better.
- The current ratio is a crude measure of solvency and in this case it has more than doubled from 1.18 in the previous year to 3.62.
- The components that make up the current assets need to be looked at to determine liquidity.
- The cash balance of £167,000 is an increase of £967,000 from the overdraft of £800,000 in the previous year, which is a strong indicator of improved liquidity.

**The trade receivables have increased by 92.76% which supports the conclusion of overtrading.**

- Trade receivables have increased by 7.8% (£87,000 / £1,115,000), not the 92.76% stated.
- This does not indicate overtrading as sales revenue has increased by 25.14%, the trade receivables collection period must be considered to determine whether or not the company is overtrading.
- The trade receivables collection period has fallen from 85.05 days in the previous year to 73.27 days, a fall of almost 12 days.
- This would indicate an improvement in credit control procedures.

**The trade payables have increased by £84,000 which indicates the company is not paying its suppliers.**

- It is correct that the trade payables have increased by £84,000.
- This is not unusual given that the cost of sales has increased by a similar proportion. The gross profit margin has remained constant which would suggest that suppliers have not increased their prices.
- The trade payables payment period has fallen slightly, but it is still significantly lower than the trade receivables collection period.

**The inventory has increased by £74,000 which supports the conclusion of overtrading.**

- Although inventory has increased it is not correct to say that this supports the conclusion of overtrading.
- Sales revenue has increased significantly and an increase in inventory would therefore also be expected.
- The increase in inventory has meant that a further £74,000 of working capital has been required.
- The inventory holding period has remained constant at 41 days which is a positive sign.

**Gearing has decreased which means that the banks are not happy to lend money to the business.**

- You are correct in stating that gearing has decreased, in this case from 52% in the previous year to 38.18%.
- This does not necessarily mean that the banks are unhappy to lend to the business, it may mean that the business does not need to increase the level of borrowing.
- The profile of debt has improved by converting a short-term overdraft of £800,000 to a long-term loan of £550,000 and an injection of capital from shareholders of £250,000.
- This has aided liquidity, but may defer cash flow problems to future years.

**(b)**    Recommendation: Yes – extended credit should be given.

**Task 6**

**(a)   Bronson Ltd**

(a) Credit Bronson Ltd's account with £9,600 and debit unallocated payments with £9,600

**(b)   Rednap Ltd**

(b) The account is not overdue so no action is required

**(c)   Hathaway Ltd**

(c) Send a copy of the signed delivery note which was signed by Hathaway Ltd

**(d)   Winslet Ltd**

(a) Winslet Ltd should be contacted to confirm which invoices are being paid so that the unallocated receipt can be allocated

**(e)   Klunee Ltd**

Contact the credit insurer to make a claim for **£28,480**, make a provision for **£7,120** and claim VAT of **£7,120** from HMRC.

**(f)   Taylor Ltd**

(d) Contact the insolvency practitioner and register a claim with the credit insurer

**Task 7**

**(a)   Downside Ltd**

- The invoice is not overdue, however the fact that the company is now is administration is a worrying sign and the account should be put on stop
- A reminder telephone call should be made on 7 October 20X3 and an overdue letter sent on 14 October 20X3 if no payment is made
- Contact the administrator of Downside Ltd and establish the likelihood of the account being paid
- It will not be possible to instigate legal proceedings whilst the company is in administration
- If the debt remains unpaid at the end of November 20X3 make a provision in the accounts

**Whistle Ltd**

- The liquidator should be contacted and Snowden Ltd must insist that they should be able to visit the premises of Whistle Ltd to attempt to identify the goods supplied by Snowden Ltd
- The threat of legal action can be made if the liquidator does not allow the visit
- The VAT of £900 should be reclaimed from HMRC
- The credit insurer should be contacted and a claim made for £3,150
- An allowance for an irrecoverable debt of £1,350 should be made in the accounts

**Vanilla Ltd**

- There is no evidence of the order, however there is evidence of the delivery and the goods were accepted by Vanilla Ltd, so somewhere a mix up has been made
- In order to maintain a good relationship with Vanilla Ltd the goods should be picked up from Vanilla Ltd and no charge made
- A credit note should be raised against the invoice

**(b)** **Mountain Ltd**

Balance at 31 August 20X3 = £10,920

Balance at 30 September 20X3 = £4,760

**Note that** the question asks for a calculation of the balances of the account at the end of the two months. This may either be carried out as a straight arithmetic exercise, or it can be done by completing two 'T' accounts as shown below.

| Dr | | | **Mountain Limited** | | | Cr |
|---|---|---|---|---|---|---|
| | | £ | | | | £ |
| 1 Aug | B/d | 45,000 | | | | |
| 2 Aug | Invoice | 12,000 | 6 Aug | Credit Note | 1,080 |
| | | | 16 Aug | Bank | 45,000 |
| | | | 31 Aug | C/d | 10,920 |
| | | 57,000 | | | 57,000 |

| Dr | | | **Mountain Limited** | | | Cr |
|---|---|---|---|---|---|---|
| | | £ | | | | £ |
| 1 Sept | B/d | 10,920 | 16 Sept | Bank | 10,000 |
| 24 Sept | Invoice | 3,840 | | | |
| | | | 30 Sept | C/d | 4,760 |
| | | 14,760 | | | 14,760 |

**(c)** **Chute Ltd**

- The first order which was invoiced on 15 March 20X3 should not have been accepted as the amount is over the credit limit for Chute Ltd
- A reminder telephone call should have been made on 21 April 20X3 for the first invoice totalling £36,000
- An overdue letter should have been sent on 28 April 20X3 for the first invoice
- The second order should not have been accepted as the account had already exceeded its credit limit
- The account should have been put on stop on 12 May 20X3
- For the second invoice totalling £28,800 a reminder telephone call should have been made on 11 June 20X3
- An overdue letter should have been sent on 18 June 20X3 for the second invoice

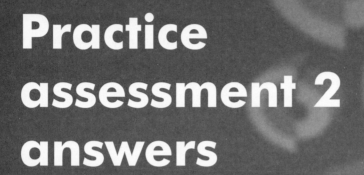

# Practice assessment 2 answers

**Task 1**

   **(a)**   (a)   When a time limit fixed for acceptance has expired

           (c)   By the buyer making a counter offer

   **(b)**   (a)   The agreement can be enforced in a court of law if necessary

   **(c)**   (b)   When there are conditions in the small print of a contract which a court of law would find unreasonable

   **(d)**   (b)   An invitation to treat

   **(e)**   (b)   No acceptance

   **(f)**   (a)   Taking legal action in the courts for recovery of an unpaid debt

   **(g)**   9 per cent

   **(h)**   £96.16

   **(i)**   The Consumer Credit Act regulates most agreements for the **granting of credit**. These include **credit sale agreements** where ownership passes to the purchaser straightaway on purchase and also **hire purchase agreements** where the consumer pays instalments to hire the item but will only take **ownership** when the final instalment has been paid.

**Task 2**

   **(a)**   (c)   Supplier trade references

   **(b)**   (a)   Factoring

   **(c)**   (c)   As there was no defined offer or acceptance there is unlikely to be a contract and so no remedies are likely to succeed

   **(d)**   (b)   An order for the court bailiffs to seize goods belonging to the seller and held by a customer who owes money to the seller

   **(e)**   (a)   A sole trader

   **(f)**   (c)   £750

   **(g)**   (b)   Appointed by a bank under its floating charge and is authorised to sell the secured assets of the company in order to repay the bank borrowing in preference to unsecured trade payables

   **(h)**   24.83% per cent

   **(i)**   38 days

**Task 3**

(a)

| SKP Limited | 20X2 Indicator | 20X2 Rating | 20X1 Indicator | 20X1 Rating |
|---|---|---|---|---|
| Profit from operations margin % | −16 | −5 | 4 | 0 |
| Interest cover | No cover | −30 | 6.4 | 10 |
| Current ratio | 1.3 | 0 | 1.5 | 10 |
| Gearing % | 76.65 | −40 | 46.67 | 10 |
| Total credit rating | | −75 | | 30 |

**Workings**:

| | Formula | 20X4 | 20X3 |
|---|---|---|---|
| Profit from operations margin % | $\dfrac{\text{Profit from operations} \times 100}{\text{Sales revenue}}$ | $\dfrac{(250,400) \times 100}{1,565,000} = -16\%$ | $\dfrac{71,360 \times 100}{1,784,000} = 4\%$ |
| Interest cover | $\dfrac{\text{Profit from operations}}{\text{Interest payable}}$ | No cover | $\dfrac{71,360}{11,150} = 6.4$ |
| Current ratio | $\dfrac{\text{Current assets}}{\text{Current liabilities}}$ | $\dfrac{387,075}{297,750} = 1.3$ | $\dfrac{274,125}{182,750} = 1.5$ |
| Gearing % | $\dfrac{\text{Total debt} \times 100}{\text{Total debt plus equity}}$ | $\dfrac{450,000 \times 100}{450,000 + 137,080} = 76.65\%$ | $\dfrac{350,000 \times 100}{350,000 + 400,000} = 46.67\%$ |

**(b)**   (b)    Reject

**Task 4**

(a)

| Weber Limited | 20X4 Indicator | 20X3 Indicator |
|---|---|---|
| Gross profit margin % | 60.96 | 60 |
| Profit from operations margin % | 21.74 | 20.25 |
| Trade payables payment period in days | 58.14 | 59.21 |
| Inventory holding period in days | 35.4 | 35.12 |
| Current ratio | 3.46 | 3.5 |
| Quick ratio | 2.85 | 2.9 |

**Workings**:

| | Formula | 20X4 | 20X3 |
|---|---|---|---|
| Gross profit margin % | $\dfrac{\text{Gross profit} \times 100}{\text{Sales revenue}}$ | $\dfrac{2{,}431 \times 100}{3{,}998} = 60.96\%$ | $\dfrac{2{,}136 \times 100}{3{,}560} = 60\%$ |
| Profit from operations margin % | $\dfrac{\text{Profit from operations} \times 100}{\text{Sales revenue}}$ | $\dfrac{867 \times 100}{3{,}988} = 21.74\%$ | $\dfrac{721 \times 100}{3{,}560} = 20.25\%$ |
| Trade payables pmt period in days | $\dfrac{\text{Trade payables} \times 365}{\text{Cost of sales}}$ | $\dfrac{248 \times 365}{1{,}557} = 58.14$ | $\dfrac{231 \times 365}{1{,}424} = 59.21$ |
| Inventory holding period in days | $\dfrac{\text{Inventories} \times 365}{\text{Cost of sales}}$ | $\dfrac{151 \times 365}{1{,}557} = 35.4$ | $\dfrac{137 \times 365}{1{,}424} = 35.12$ |
| Current ratio | $\dfrac{\text{Current assets}}{\text{Current liabilities}}$ | $\dfrac{858}{248} = 3.46$ | $\dfrac{808}{231} = 3.5$ |
| Quick ratio | $\dfrac{\text{Current assets less inventories}}{\text{Current liabilities}}$ | $\dfrac{858 - 151}{248} = 2.85$ | $\dfrac{808 - 137}{231} = 2.9$ |

**(b)** (1) Sales revenue for 20X4 compared to 20X3 has increased by **12.02%** which means that the company may have **experienced an increased demand for its products.**

(2) The gross profit margin has remained constant, which indicates that the company has **made no change to the selling and purchase price of its product**.

(3) The company is making a **profit** at operational level and the profit from operations margin has **increased**.

(4) The trade payables payment period measures on average the number of days that **the company takes to pay its suppliers**. For Weber Ltd this has **fallen** slightly.

(5) The current ratio is **greater than 1**, which is a **good sign**.

(6) The quick ratio is **more than 1** which **is not** a major concern in terms of liquidity.

(7) The inventory holding period has remained constant. This is a **good sign** and indicates **stability**.

(8) Overall it appears that the company is **solvent** and has **sufficient** liquidity to pays its liabilities as they fall due.

(9) On the basis of the financial statements that have been provided to us and the key performance indicators, I recommend that **credit be given** to Weber Ltd.

**Workings:**

(1) Increase in revenue (3,988 − 3,560) / 3,560 = 12.02%

**Task 5 (a)**

**The company turnover has increased by 44.34% from £5.9 million to £10.6 million. This is an excellent sign which shows that the company is expanding.**

- You are correct that the turnover has increased, but the increase is 79.66% (£4,700,000 / £5,900,000), not 44.34%.

- The fact that turnover has increased significantly may be a sign of overtrading, but other indicators have to be considered.

- These include significant increases in turnover linked to reduced margins, increased levels of current assets and trade cycle days and cash reduction in flow.

- These points will be considered below.

**The gross profit has increased from £2,006,000 to £2,809,000. This means that more cash is available to pay debts.**

- You are correct that the gross profit has increased by £803,000; however, the gross profit margin has fallen by 7.5% from 34% to 26.5%, which would indicate that suppliers may have increased their prices.

- An increase in gross profit does not mean that more cash is available to pay debts; it depends on where the profit has gone in the period.

- Has it been "invested" or is it "tied up" in inventory, trade receivables or non-current assets?

- This is why it is necessary to consider the liquidity of the business and changes in the assets and liabilities to confirm the liquidity of the business.

**The profit from operations has increased by £138,000 and the profit after tax has remained the same which is a good sign.**

- The profit from operations has increased, but as with the gross profit margin the profit from operations margin has also fallen from 19.27% to 12.03%, a fall of just over 7%.

- This would indicate that the administration and distribution expenses have risen at roughly the same rate as turnover.

- Profit after tax has remained roughly the same due to a significant increase in finance costs.

**The interest cover is now much better than the previous year, when it was too high.**

- Interest cover has fallen from 63 times in the previous year to just below 7 times.

- Interest cover is a key indicator that is often used by credit agencies and financial institutions to calculate how many times the profit from operations can cover the interest payments.

- The calculation of 6.82 times indicates that the interest paid is covered by the profit from operations by almost 7 times.

- The big reduction in interest cover is due to the company now having a large overdraft which it did not have in the previous year.

- Cash generation is needed to pay interest. Many profitable companies fail because they cannot generate cash to pay their liabilities as they fall due.

**The current ratio has fallen, but it is still over 1 which means the company is solvent.**

- Referring to the fact that the current ratio is over 1 and therefore the company is solvent is a common misunderstanding; an unacceptable current ratio very much depends on the organisation itself and the type of industry to which it belongs.

- A higher current ratio indicates a better credit worthiness when assessing a potential credit customer.
- The current ratio is a crude measure of solvency and in this case it has decreased significantly from 5.31 in the previous year to 1.42, which may indicate insolvency.
- The components that make up current assets need to be looked at to determine liquidity.
- The cash balance has fallen by £1,482,000 and the company now places a heavy reliance on a short-term overdraft which could be an increased risk to the business.

**The trade receivables have increased by £1,899,000 which is a good sign as it is far less than the increase in turnover of £4,700,000.**

- Trade receivables have increased from £947,000 to £2,846,000; an increase would be expected with the significant increase in sales revenues.
- However, the collection period has increased by almost 40 days. This would indicate that the company's Credit Control Department is struggling to collect debts and may also point to overtrading.

**The trade payables payment period has increased from 42 days to 83 days; this implies that the company is taking advantage of good credit terms from suppliers.**

- The trade payables have increased by £1,324,000; an increase would be expected and there has been a significant increase in cost of sales.
- The increase in the trade payables payment period from 42 to 83 days is not a good sign. It indicates that the company is struggling to pay suppliers on time and is another strong indicator of overtrading.

**The inventory has remained the same which is an excellent sign.**

- Inventory levels have remained roughly the same compared to last year which is not necessarily a good sign.
- The inventory holding period has decreased from 60.93 days to 30.55 days, which may indicate that the business is unable to buy further inventory and could mean that inventory may well run out.

**Gearing has increased which means that the banks are happy to lend money to this business.**

- There is an increase in the level of gearing from 26.33% to 43.17%.
- This is as a result of the significant bank overdraft the business now has.
- There has been a fall in the long term borrowing which may mean that banks are not happy to lend the company money over a long period.
- The increase in the bank overdraft has been used to fund the working capital of the business; there has been no investment in non-current assets.

**(b)** No - you would not recommend granting the increase in credit limit to Lily Limited.

## Task 6

**(a)** **Tilsley Ltd**

(a) The account should be put on stop

**(b)** **Cole Ltd**

(b) The account is not overdue so no action is required

**(c)** **McDonald Ltd**

(d) Contact the insolvency practitioner and make a provision in the accounts

**(d)** **Lloyd Ltd**

(a) Lloyd Ltd should be contacted to confirm which invoices are being paid so that the unallocated receipt can be allocated

**(e)** **Grimshaw Ltd**

Contact the credit insurer to make a claim for **£0**, make a provision for **£15,000** and claim VAT of **£3,000** from HMRC.

**(f)** **Duckworth Ltd**

(b) Ask the Managing Director of Barlow Ltd what action should be taken

## Task 7

**(a)** **Magnum Ltd**
- The account should have been put on stop because it is more than 28 days overdue
- A member of staff should visit the premises of Magnum Ltd and ask for immediate payment
- The debt should be placed in the hands of a debt collection agency if the visit proves to be unsuccessful
- A claim of £9,100 should be made from the insurer (ie 70% of the net invoice amount)
- Once the debt is over six months old Bad Debt Relief of £2,600 should be claimed from HMRC
- A provision of £3,900 should be made in the accounts

**Hudsons Inc**
- Additional care must be taken with foreign customers as they may take longer to settle invoices and allowing them to exceed their credit limit would not be advisable
- Hudsons Inc must be contacted and asked for settlement of the £25,000 before the new order of £35,000 can be processed

**Shoreline Ltd**
- For the invoice dated 30 June 20X3 use the normal credit control process which will be a telephone call on 7 August 20X3 followed by a letter on 14 August 20X3
- For the invoice dated 31 May 20X3 contact Shoreline Ltd and ask why the payment has not been made yet
- As Shoreline Ltd usually pays on time it is possible that the older invoice is in dispute or that the payment has been lost or misposted
- It is not necessary at this stage to make any provision in the accounts

**(b)** Balance at 30 June 20X3 = £72,000

Balance at 31 July 20X3 = £61,680

**Note that** the question asks for a calculation of the balances of the account at the end of the two months. This may either be carried out as a straight arithmetic exercise, or it can be done by completing two 'T' accounts as shown below.

| Dr | | **Sheila Mary Ltd** | | | | Cr |
|---|---|---|---|---|---|---|
| | | £ | | | | £ |
| 1 Jun | B/d | 165,000 | | | | |
| 8 Jun | Invoice | 72,000 | 5 Jun | Bank | 162,000 |
| | | | 6 Jun | Credit note | 3,000 |
| | | | 30 Jun | C/d | 72,000 |
| | | 237,000 | | | 237,000 |

| Dr | | **Sheila Mary Ltd** | | | | Cr |
|---|---|---|---|---|---|---|
| | | £ | | | | £ |
| 1 Jul | B/d | 72,000 | | | | |
| 15 Jul | Invoice | 67,200 | 17 Jul | Credit note | 5,520 |
| | | | 20 Jul | Bank | 72,000 |
| | | | 31 Jul | C/d | 61,680 |
| | | 139,200 | | | 139,200 |

**(c)** **Sweet Pea Ltd**
- The second invoice dated 1 June 20X3 should not have been accepted as this meant that Sweet Pea Ltd exceeded its credit limit
- The first invoice totalling £6,000 should have had a reminder telephone call on 7 June 20X3
- The first invoice should then have had an overdue letter on 14 June 20X3
- The account should have been put on stop on 28 June 20X3 due to non-payment of the first invoice
- The second invoice totalling £19,200 should have had a reminder telephone call on 8 July 20X3
- There should have been an overdue letter on 15 July 20X3 for the second invoice

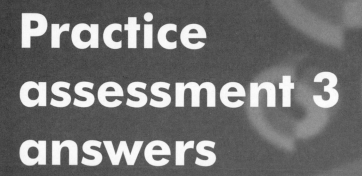

# Practice assessment 3 answers

**Task 1**

    **(a)**    (a)    Unconditional

    **(b)**    (a)    A counter offer is made

    **(c)**    (a)    Only individuals

    **(d)**    (a)    The £5 is sufficient consideration even if a very low price is set as a favour to the buyer

    **(e)**    (a)    There is no valid contract because the agreement was a domestic one and not intended to create legal relations

    **(f)**    (b)    A person who takes legal action in the courts for money compensation for breach of contract

    **(g)**    9.25 per cent

    **(h)**    £131.18

    **(i)**    The Sale of Goods Act states that any purchaser should expect goods purchased to be of **satisfactory quality**, as **described** and **fit for the purpose**. Title to the goods passes to the purchaser when the parties to the contract **intend** that it should, normally this will be on **delivery**.

**Task 2**

    **(a)**    (a)    The bank is not fully sure and hints that further enquiries should be made

    **(b)**    (c)    Contact the customer by telephone and discuss the matter

    **(c)**    (b)    Fast Track

    **(d)**    (c)    An order for the court bailiffs to seize goods belonging to the seller and held by a customer who owes money to the seller

    **(e)**    (c)    A formal demand for at least £750 made by the person or company owed money

    **(f)**    (a)    An individual

    **(g)**    (c)    Try to recover the money and hope that the company recovers

    **(h)**    40.69 per cent

    **(i)**    41 days

**Task 3**

(a)

| Garden Design Limited | 20X2 Indicator | 20X2 Rating | 20X1 Indicator | 20X1 Rating |
|---|---|---|---|---|
| Profit from operations margin % | 15 | 10 | –4 | –5 |
| Interest cover | 32.14 | 10 | No cover | –30 |
| Quick ratio | 2.23 | 10 | 3.47 | 10 |
| Gearing % | 34.97 | 10 | 65.71 | –20 |
| Total credit rating | | 40 | | –45 |

**Workings**:

| | Formula | 20X2 | 20X1 |
|---|---|---|---|
| Profit from operations margin % | $\dfrac{\text{Profit from operations} \times 100}{\text{Sales revenue}}$ | $\dfrac{1{,}125 \times 100}{7{,}500} = 15\%$ | $\dfrac{252 \times 100}{6{,}300} = -4\%$ |
| Interest cover | $\dfrac{\text{Profit from operations}}{\text{Interest payable}}$ | $\dfrac{1{,}125}{35} = 32.14$ | No cover |
| Quick ratio | $\dfrac{\text{Current assets less inventories}}{\text{Current liabilities}}$ | $\dfrac{1{,}427 - 151}{571} = 2.23$ | $\dfrac{1{,}632 - 148}{428} = 3.47$ |
| Gearing % | $\dfrac{\text{Total debt} \times 100}{\text{Total debt plus equity}}$ | $\dfrac{1{,}000 \times 100}{1{,}000 + 1{,}860} = 34.97\%$ | $\dfrac{1{,}600 \times 100}{1{,}600 + 835} = 65.71\%$ |

(b)   (c)   Request latest management accounts and defer decision.

**Task 4**

(a)

| Joseph Limited | 20X3 Indicator | 20X2 Indicator |
|---|---|---|
| Gross profit margin % | 30.05 | 29.83 |
| Profit from operations margin % | 10.04 | 9.9 |
| Trade payables payment period in days | 90.99 | 56.07 |
| Inventory holding period in days | 27.95 | 44.95 |
| Current ratio | 0.9 | 1.75 |
| Quick ratio | 0.61 | 0.94 |

**Workings**:

| | Formula | 20X3 | 20X2 |
|---|---|---|---|
| Gross profit margin % | $\dfrac{\text{Gross profit} \times 100}{\text{Sales revenue}}$ | $\dfrac{1{,}840 \times 100}{6{,}124} = 30.05\%$ | $\dfrac{1{,}353 \times 100}{4{,}536} = 29.83\%$ |
| Profit from operations margin % | $\dfrac{\text{Profit from operations} \times 100}{\text{Sales revenue}}$ | $\dfrac{615 \times 100}{6{,}124} = 10.04\%$ | $\dfrac{449 \times 100}{4{,}536} = 9.9\%$ |
| Trade payables pmt period in days | $\dfrac{\text{Trade payables} \times 365}{\text{Cost of sales}}$ | $\dfrac{1{,}068 \times 365}{4{,}284} = 90.99$ | $\dfrac{489 \times 365}{3{,}183} = 56.07$ |
| Inventory holding period in days | $\dfrac{\text{Inventories} \times 365}{\text{Cost of sales}}$ | $\dfrac{328 \times 365}{4{,}284} = 27.95$ | $\dfrac{392 \times 365}{3{,}183} = 44.95$ |
| Current ratio | $\dfrac{\text{Current assets}}{\text{Current liabilities}}$ | $\dfrac{1{,}012}{56 + 1{,}068} = 0.9$ | $\dfrac{854}{489} = 1.75$ |
| Quick ratio | $\dfrac{\text{Current assets less inventories}}{\text{Current liabilities}}$ | $\dfrac{1{,}012 - 328}{56 + 1{,}068} = 0.61$ | $\dfrac{854 - 392}{489} = 0.94$ |

**(b)**

(1)    Sales revenue for 20X3 compared to 20X2 has increased by **35.01%**, which means that the company may have **either sold more units or increased the selling price of its product**.

(2)    Gross profit has increased by **35.99%** and profit from operations has increased by **36.97%**. Both the gross profit margin and the profit from operations margin have **increased** slightly.

(3)    The current ratio provides a rough measure of the **short-term solvency** of the organisation. In the case of Joseph Ltd it has **fallen** and is now **less than 1**, which is a **sign of poor liquidity**.

(4)    The inventory level has **decreased**; this is a **bad sign** as the inventory holding period has **decreased**, which may mean that **inventory could run out**.

(5)    The quick ratio has **fallen** which **is** a major concern and indicates **poor** liquidity.

(6)    The trade payables payment period has **increased** by **34.92** days. It appears that the company is **finding it more difficult** to pay its liabilities as they fall due.

(7)    On the basis of the financial statements that have been provided to us and the key performance indicators I recommend that **credit not be given** to Joseph Limited.

**Workings:**

(1)    Increase in revenue                               (6,124 – 4,536) / 4,536 = 35.01%

(2)    Increase in gross profit                          (1,840 – 1,353) / 1,353 = 35.99%

(2)    Increase in profit from operations       (615 – 449) / 449 = 36.97%

(6)    Increase in trade payables payment days    90.99 – 56.07 = 34.92 days

## Task 5 (a)

**The company turnover has increased by 13.01% from £4,575,000 to £5,170,000. This is a good sign.**

- You are correct that the turnover has increased by 13.01%, whether or not it is a good sign depends on other factors.
- These include significant increases in turnover linked to reduced margins, increased levels of current assets and trade cycle days and a reduction in cash flow.
- These points will be considered below.

**The profit from operations has decreased by £768,000. This means that less cash is available to pay debts.**

- You are correct that the profit from operations has fallen and in 20X2 there is an operating loss.
- What is of concern is that whilst the gross profit margin has remained constant at 60% the profit from operations margin has fallen from 10.99% to –5.13%.
- A decrease in the profit from operations does not mean that less cash is available to pay debts; it depends on where the profit has gone in the period.
- Has it been "invested" or is it "tied up" in inventory, trade receivables or non-current assets?
- This is why it is necessary to consider the liquidity of the business and changes in the assets and liabilities to confirm the liquidity of the business.
- The administration expenses have increased from 37.01% of sales revenue to 53.13% of sales revenue which has contributed to the operating loss.
- There has been a significant increase in administration expenses. This figure will include depreciation which will have increased due to the large investment in non-current assets.

**There is no interest cover which means that the company is in a worse position than last year.**

- Interest cover was over 50 times in the previous year and now there is no cover, as the company no longer has any borrowing commitments which attract interest.
- There appears to have been a significant injection of capital from shareholders, part of which has been used to pay back the long term loan.

**The current ratio should be 2 which means in both years it is too high.**

- Referring to the fact that the business's current ratio should be 2 is a common misunderstanding; it very much depends on the organisation itself and the type of industry in which it operates.
- Generally, the higher the current ratio the better from an assessment of credit perspective.
- The current ratio is a crude measure of solvency and in this case it has increased from 4.38 in the previous year to 5.36, which is a positive sign.
- The components of the current assets figure need to be looked at further to determine liquidity.
- The cash balance has increased by £66,000 which again is a positive sign.

**The trade receivables have increased by £82,000 which means the company is overtrading.**

- Trade receivables have increased from £626,000 to £708,000; an increase would be expected with the increase in sales revenues.
- The collection period has remained constant which is a good sign.

**The trade payables payment period is down from 49.07 days to 40.95 days which implies that the company is struggling to obtain credit from its suppliers.**

- Trade payables have decreased and the payment period has also decreased.

- This does not necessarily indicate that the company is struggling to get credit from suppliers; it indicates that the company is moving towards paying suppliers within the usual 30 days.

**Inventory has increased which supports the conclusion of overtrading.**

- Inventory levels have increased in line with the increase in cost of sales.

- The inventory holding period has decreased slightly from 53.05 days to 49.95 days, which is an indicator that inventory may be being used more efficiently.

**Gearing has decreased which means that the banks are not happy to lend money to the business.**

- There is a decrease in gearing from 10.59% to nothing, which may be an indicator that the banks are no longer prepared to lend the business money. Alternatively, it may simply be that the business no longer has any borrowing requirements.

- There has been a large change in equity with an injection of capital of £2.6 million.

- The capital appears to have funded the purchase of non-current assets and repayment of the long-term loan.

**(b)** (c)   Request up-to-date management accounts and details of the equity injection made in 20X2 before granting credit

**Task 6**

(a)  **Clarke Ltd**

(c) A final reminder letter should be sent on 4 November 20X3

(b)  **Day Ltd**

(b) Establish that the payment was from Day Ltd, credit Day Ltd with £17,400 and debit unallocated payments with £17,400

(c)  **Horwood Ltd**

(c) Contact the insolvency practitioner and register a claim with the credit insurer

(d)  **Rhodes Ltd**

(c) Refer the debt to a debt collection agency and make a provision in the accounts

(e)  **Stein Ltd**

(b) The account is not overdue so no action is required

**Task 7**

(a)  **Beck Ltd**
   - Ensure that the account has been put on stop
   - Establish why Beck Ltd is refusing to pay
   - Establish if Beck Ltd still has the goods to which this debt relates and if so reclaim them under the retention of title clause
   - Consider taking legal action if the goods cannot be identified
   - Make a provision in the accounts for £750
   - Make a claim with the insurers for £1,750
   - Claim £500 back from HMRC when the debt is over six months old

**Free Ltd**
   - The products which have been manufactured by Opto Ltd have a batch number, therefore they should be separately identifiable from other products
   - A member of staff should visit the premises of Free Ltd to identify the products supplied in the presence of the receiver
   - A claim should be made from the insurer for £8,750
   - The VAT of £2,500 is reclaimable from HMRC
   - A provision of £3,750 should be made in the accounts

**Hardy Ltd**
   - The premises of Hardy Ltd should be visited to establish whether or not the company is still trading
   - A provision should be made in the accounts for the full amount of the debt less VAT as the debt will not be credit insured
   - VAT can be reclaimed from HMRC
   - A debt collection company should be engaged to pursue the matter further

**(b)** **Monte Ltd**

Balance at 31 May 20X3 = £36,800
[105,000 + (40,000 x 1.2) – (18,000 x 90%) – 100,000 = 36,800]

Balance at 30 June 20X3 = £80,000
[36,800 – 30,000 + 78,000 – 4,800 = 80,000]

**Note:** T-accounts are also shown as possible workings below.

| Dr | | | Monte Ltd | | Cr |
|---|---|---|---|---|---|
| | | £ | | | £ |
| 1 May | B/d | 105,000 | | | |
| 8 May | Invoice | 48,000 | 10 May | Credit note | 16,200 |
| | | | 10 May | Bank | 100,000 |
| | | | 31 May | C/d | 36,800 |
| | | 153,000 | | | 153,000 |

| Dr | | | Monte Ltd | | Cr |
|---|---|---|---|---|---|
| | | £ | | | £ |
| 1 Jun | B/d | 36,800 | | | |
| 16 Jun | Invoice | 78,000 | 10 Jun | Bank | 30,000 |
| | | | 26 Jun | Credit note | 4,800 |
| | | | 30 Jun | C/d | 80,000 |
| | | 114,800 | | | 114,800 |

**(c)** **Oliver Ltd**

- The first invoice totalling £3,600 should have had a telephone reminder on 7 April 20X3
- The first invoice should have had an overdue letter on 14 April 20X3
- The account should have been put on stop on 28 April 20X3
- The order relating to the second invoice should not have been accepted due to the account being on stop
- The second invoice totalling £3,000 should have had a telephone reminder on 8 June 20X3
- The second invoice should have had an overdue letter on 15 June 20X3

for your notes

**for your notes**

**for your notes**

for your notes

for your notes